SALLY MORGAN ENTERTAINMENTS

Call Me Psychic

D0995195

Call Me Psychic

SALLY MORGAN

SALLY MORGAN ENTERTAINMENTS

SALLY MORGAN ENTERTAINMENTS LTD

Published by Sally Morgan entertainments Limited

Sally Morgan entertainments LTD, Reigate business centre,
7-11 High Street, Reigate, RH2 9AA

Sally Morgan Entertainments Ltd, Registered offices: 3rd Floor Aissela
42-50 High Street, Esher, Surrey, KT10 9QY.

www.sallymorgan.tv

First Published 2015

Set in 12.5/14.75pt Garamond MT Std
Typeset in England by CPI Typesetting
Printed and bound by CPI Group (UK) Ltd, Croydon, CR0 4YY

Some Names, locations and details have been changed to
protect the identities and the privacy of the individuals involved

ISBN 978-0-9927001-9-5

Contents

In loving memory of my darling
"Unc Unc " Derek George Comyns.

A wonderful caring uncle, husband,
father and a great friend to many.

I will be forever grateful for his
unending support of my work, which
he was very proud of. Encouraging me
to continue exploring my gift.

5th November 1938 – 4th March 2015.

Author's note

I've always thought that people who write autobiography after autobiography are a bit weird. And then I was given the opportunity to write my second life story and realised that since my first book was published so much has happened it's as if I've lived another life so I jumped at the chance and it didn't seem like a strange thing to do after all.

My first autobiography, *My Psychic Life*, was published in 2008 and it's all about my upbringing and explains how I became Britain's best-known medium. I wrote that book when I was in my mid-fifties. When I'd finished I thought to myself, 'That'll do. I'm settled now, what more can happen?' But it turns out that was just half the story.

Since then everything has changed. My work has changed, my body has changed, my relationships have changed and I've changed too. And that's what this book is about: my second life.

Writing a life story is cathartic. It's like going to see a therapist – you reflect for hours, at times it's a difficult process and you dredge up things you'd rather not have to confront again. Other times you find things you think you have lost and you get shocked by certain things you remember.

I'd like to thank my family for their unswerving

support through the times detailed in this story and for staying strong when times were tough. I'd also like to thank Nick Harding for his help and expertise.

Sally Morgan, 2015

4

Chapter 1
A star psychic is born

'It's a wrap!'

The director mimed a cutting motion across his neck and smiled. The red light on top of the camera blinked out. And that was it: my first ever TV series was over. I stood there in front of the cameraman, kicking my heels.

'Er, what else do you need me to do?' I asked.

'Nothing, Sal, it's in the bag.'

It was early 2007 and I'd just finished filming a psychic reading for my new TV show, *Sally Morgan: Star Psychic*. The last few months had been madness as we rushed to get enough footage for the five shows that were due to be broadcast on ITV2 that March. This was my first dip into the world of television after running a successful medium practice from my home in suburban Surrey for the previous three and a half decades and my feet hadn't touched the ground. It had been a whirlwind of early mornings, late nights and psychic challenges. I'd met loads of people, I'd reduced some celebs to tears with the accuracy of my readings and converted more than a few cynics along the way.

I'd just finished a reading for Rhona Cameron, the Scottish comedienne who'd been in the first series of ITV's *I'm A Celebrity... Get Me Out Of Here!* At the beginning Rhona was very sceptical; she simply didn't believe that I could communicate with the dead. And logically, who could blame her? It was quite a statement to make. But then logic never stopped me in the past and as the reading progressed she couldn't deny that something amazing was happening. When someone is closed to the possibility of a life after death it can be tricky to connect with the psychic energy around them and their cynicism usually acts as a barrier but for some reason the messages for Rhona came fast; I got hit after hit. I saw she had two dogs in spirit and I picked up their names. I also got the names and details of her dead relatives who had come through for her to try and encourage her to be more accepting. In the end she was in tears; it was an emotional reading and we were both drained.

The show's tagline was '*30 Celebrities. 30 Challenges. 30 Days. 1 Psychic*'. Filming had been as hectic as the description suggested and I was now mentally, physically and emotionally exhausted. When it was over I flagged. The excitement and adrenaline of having a TV show had kept me going but once that camera switched off for the last time I felt my whole body and brain slump. The end was a huge anti-climax. I don't know what I was expecting. Applause? Flowers? A congratulatory telegram from HM the Queen? Instead I climbed into the people carrier that had ferried me between locations over the previous weeks and was driven home. We stopped briefly at M&S on the way so I could grab a sandwich and an iced bun.

In the short period between the end of filming and the show being broadcast I almost forgot what had happened. It's amazing how quickly I adjusted back to normal life. We all do it – we go on holiday, have an amazing time and even though we're gone for just a week or two, we imagine everything will be different when we return. It rarely is, and we trudge back to our lives. Within days it's as if nothing ever happened.

It was the same for me. When the show did start to get some publicity and promotion it took me by surprise. One night I saw a trailer for it when I was watching telly and recognised the lady on the screen with the high-pitched voice: it was me!

Star Psychic was first shown on a Thursday night and my husband John and I invited a few family and friends round to watch. We popped a bottle of champagne and sat in the lounge of our house in Motspur Park, Surrey, waiting for the opening credits to roll. My stomach churned and when I heard the theme tune I squealed. I then spent the next 30 minutes peeking at the screen from between my fingers while John and our guests gently poked fun at me. It was clear at that early stage that no matter how my fledgling television career progressed, those nearest and dearest to me would never allow me to get too big for my boots.

My circumstances were the same as they were before the TV show – I lived in the house, did the same job, shopped in the same supermarket – but over the following days I started to realise that being on television was going to change my life in ways I hadn't considered. Life would jog along as normal and then something would happen to jolt me into the realisation that I was a recognisable figure: I was a woman off the telly! I remember vividly the first time I was recognised. It was a couple of days after that first show and John, who is an avid Fulham FC fan, had gone to watch a game. It was late afternoon and I'd nipped into Tesco to get something for dinner.

It was getting dark and I parked up in the dimly lit car park. It was one of those huge Tesco Extra 24-hour megastores so there was plenty of traffic coming and going. As I walked towards the entrance I heard a commotion a few yards away. Glancing over, I saw a large lady waving and shrieking; she was clearly trying to get someone's attention. Momentarily I stopped, worried that something had happened, but she seemed to be smiling. I didn't sense any danger so I carried on towards the shop. The lady continued to shout and then I realised she was heading in my direction. I'm a bit deaf so I only realised what she was shouting when she was just a few metres behind me.

'Oh my God, it's *you*, Sally Morgan!'

At that point in time I'd forgotten I'd been on telly. That's the funny thing about so-called fame – it takes a while to realise you are recognisable and as you get on with your everyday life you forget that people know who you are. You just get a sense that they're looking at you and then you wonder if you've grown two heads or got your skirt tucked into your knickers by accident.

I was confused when the lady called my name and did that thing we all do when someone recognises us and we don't know who they are: I wracked my brain to try and work out where I knew her from… and then I bluffed.

'Hello, love,' I said, 'how are you?'

'I can't believe it's *you!*' she answered, gasping for breath. She'd run half the length of the car park and by the look of her she wasn't used to physical exercise.

I gave up trying to guess where I knew her from.

'I'm really sorry and I hope you don't think I'm being rude, but do I know you? Have I given you a reading in the past?' I tried.

She looked at me and frowned.

'No, I saw you on the telly. I love your show, I think you're amazing!' she gushed.

At this the penny dropped and I smiled.

'Oh yeah, of course!' I laughed. 'You'll have to excuse me, love, I'm not used to all this showbiz stuff.'

After that I didn't know what to do. I didn't know the etiquette for these situations so I just smiled at her and continued towards the doors of the store. She grabbed my arm.

'Please don't go anywhere. I need to get my sister,' she said. 'We watched your show together. She's a big fan too.'

It was at that point that I started to realise that there would be repercussions to being on television. But I was no stranger to the media – I'd been in newspapers and magazines before –having my own series was an altogether different ball game, though. And because I was a big lady, I was fairly recognisable. It sounds naive now but it really hadn't occurred to me that people would start to recognise me, talk to me in the street and try to contact me. I didn't have an agent to explain the implications and talk me through what to expect. Nowadays celebrity agents are ten a penny and someone only has to be in reality show for five minutes and the next thing they know, they have a PR agent to train them up in interview techniques. But it was different for me. For a start it didn't occur to me that I'd need anything of the sort. Until then I'd survived well enough without one so why on earth would I need an agent? And so I felt my way through the obstacle course of celebrity.

The lady in the car park had my arm in a grip. It wasn't threatening; it was purposeful. Gently I tried to extricate myself from her.

'Please, you've got to meet my sister. She only lives round the corner. I'll call her,' she insisted. With her free hand she reached into the bag slung over her shoulder and pulled out one of those old Nokia phones.

'Nah, I've got to get my shopping,' I told her. 'John will be home from football soon and I'll need to get tea on.'

Finally she let me go after I'd scribbled an autograph for her. After that it was like a veil had been lifted. As I walked up and down the aisles of the supermarket I noticed people were looking at me. In the past I'd get strange looks all the time but this was different – the looks were furtive, people would stare and think I couldn't see them. When I looked back, they looked away. It may well have been me being paranoid after the debacle in the car park but I could definitely sense a few glances of recognition. And over the following days they became increasingly common. Several more people stopped me when I was out and about to ask for an autograph but I felt silly signing them. I was just plain old me, Sally. I wasn't a celebrity, was I?

It's safe to say that over the coming weeks the impact that *Sally Morgan: Star Psychic* had on my life was like an atomic bomb going off. It changed everything and flattened everything else that it didn't change. Honestly, I never thought the show would be so successful. I believed that it would be lost somewhere in the schedules in a late-night slot and that if I was lucky, a few thousand people would watch it. After the series finished I would go back to my busy but quiet life, working from home, I thought. Up to that point I was unknown outside of the psychic circle but I was London's best-kept secret. If you went into Knightsbridge, Kensington or Chelsea and asked some of the well-heeled ladies who lived in those areas to name a famous psychic, a few of them might have mentioned me. I was known on the fringes of the aristocracy because of the high-profile clients I had, such as Princess Diana, but to the wider world I was nobody.

But that all changed very quickly. The comedian Harry Hill helped. At the time one of the most popular shows on television was his *TV Burp* programme, in which he gently took the rise out of TV shows. Harry had seen my show and decided to use me as a running joke in his series. Each week he sent me up. People asked if I was offended. Of course not! I thought Harry was hilarious and they say imitation is the most sincere form of flattery. I didn't mind his jokey impressions of me one bit – because of them more people started to recognise me.

While my life was changing, one thing stayed the same: my income. People assumed that because I was on television, I had suddenly become rich but that could not be further from the truth. For the record, in the case of both *Star Psychic* and subsequently my follow-up series, *Sally Morgan: On The Road* (which we'll come to a little later), I was paid the grand sum of… zilch! Hard to believe, isn't it? Even when *On The Road* was sold around the world and shown in loads of different countries and repeated endlessly I still received no royalties or fees. My expenses were covered, that's all. Don't get me wrong, I did not complain – I was glad of the opportunity. But people found it hard to believe that I didn't become a millionaire overnight. I did it all for free. Why? I wanted to show people that my ability existed and that I was only an ordinary person. I was keen to reach a wider audience, to enlighten people and to show them the wonders of the spirit world. It makes me laugh when I hear the phrase 'rich and famous' because those words don't always follow and in my case they certainly didn't. There was no budget for *Star Psychic* – the clothes I wore were mine, carefully picked from my own wardrobe each morning. There was no hair and make-up artist, I did it all myself. That's why I cringe when I watch it – I look such a mess!

Up until then I hadn't given the future much thought. I presumed I would carry on with my practice and I was so used to having regular work, to getting up in the morning in a routine. From start to finish I knew what I was going to be doing each day. My husband John worked with me – he was the booker, he made the appointments and organised my diary. He introduced me to the clients when they arrived at the house and made sure they were comfortable if they needed to wait. We worked together and it was a very successful arrangement. That was it, that was my life and that was how I assumed things would stay.

I was so naive about the effects of being on television that I still advertised in the Yellow Pages (for younger readers, the Yellow Pages was an extremely thick phone directory that every household had and men would sometimes attempt to rip one in half in an effort to prove how strong they were!). As a result, anyone with a southwest London directory could easily look up my phone number and my address – and they did. Soon the office phone started ringing off the hook and it never stopped; it was ringing day and night. It was John's job to answer the calls and that became a full-time job in itself. As soon as he put the receiver down, the phone rang again. Everything went mad. I've always been a grafter and I don't like turning work away so he tried desperately to fit in as many clients as he could.

'You've got six tomorrow, Sally. If you start an hour earlier and finish an hour later you could fit a few more in,' he advised.

So I started working weekends to try and keep up with the demand. It was silly – I had a major TV series but I was still trying to run my business as if I was a small independent. It became too busy and intense. I was drained and I wasn't seeing my kids or my grandchildren.

I guess you could say I became a victim of my own success. Some of the footage from the show was so explosive that everywhere I went people wanted readings. It became awkward when people in the area I lived in who I'd never spoken to (and in some cases had never even seen before) would knock on the door. If I came out of the house to get in the car, which was parked in the driveway, I'd be accosted.

'Are you that psychic woman?' they'd say. 'I've

been living here for years and I've always meant to book for a reading. Have you got five minutes?'

But it never was five minutes; it would go on and on. Very quickly I learnt two lessons. Lesson number one: unplug the phone. Lesson number two: never agree to an impromptu five-minute reading. In the end I would hide out the back of the house whenever there was someone at the door. John would have to stand in the doorway to block out the view so they couldn't see in.

'She's not here,' he'd say.

'But we just saw her walk in!' they'd insist.

Often it felt like I was being followed and to begin with, it freaked me out. Fame takes a lot of getting used to and although people will say, 'Sally, you were on TV, what did you expect?' I really had no idea what it would be like.

One fan regularly drove all the way from north London in the hope of catching me in. She'd sit in her car down the road and keep an eye on the house. She knew my car and realised that when it was in the drive, I was home. She worked out my schedule; she knew what days I went shopping and made sure she was there when I left the house. I had to change things around to try and avoid her.

I came home and notes had been put through the door from people who had randomly called and missed me. Now I was more popular than I'd ever been – I received invitations to weddings, funerals and Bar Mitzvahs, all from people I didn't know.

After the TV series I ended up with a waiting list of 72,000 people. If I'd carried on as normal I would have been able to work for 30 years without ever taking another booking! Quite clearly that was mad and something had to change but I didn't know what. I never had a five-year plan and to be honest, I was nervous about the future. However, I'm a person who loves change and I thrive on the unknown. Every New Year's Eve John and I have the same discussion.

'What do you think will happen this year?' I ask.

Inevitably he will reply: 'Let's try and keep doing what we are doing.'

But that's not what I wanted: I wanted something different in my life, I wanted to throw it up in the air and see what happened. That craving for change was something that was in me. It probably developed when I was a child. Back then for much of the time there was unhappiness in my life and I wanted to change it. The people around me were unhappy. My mum lost her mother when she was young and she grieved for years and years. As a kid I saw how sad she was and I wanted to change that and make her happy. There was turmoil and sadness. I wanted to change things for the better and so, as I grew, I embraced the changes life threw at me and tried to take advantage of everything life offered so I took risks and most of the time they paid off. When I met John at a New Year's Eve party in 1974 (another time of change), he became my perfect counterbalance because he is cautious about things – that's why we worked so well together. But as the series came to an end it was the first time in my life that I was uncertain about change. The one thing I had never been able to do with my gift was read my own fortune.

Something big was about to happen, but I had no idea what it would be.

Chapter 2
Planning ahead

I'd be lying if I said that I didn't want to do another series of *Star Psychic*, and to begin with, that was the plan. Despite all the hard work and the running around that went into making it, and despite the fact that I earned nothing from it, I loved the end result and I enjoyed the fact that it showed people what I was capable of. It also showed viewers there was more to mediums than crystal balls and headscarves. Before the show came along, the world of mediumship was old-fashioned, spooky and stuffy. I'd never been part of that psychic community. I didn't socialise with any other mediums and although I took an interest in the psychic world, I didn't follow any other celebrity mediums. Of course I knew of people such as Derek Acorah and Colin Fry. And I had the utmost respect for the late Doris Stokes, who was the grandmother of all celebrity psychics and did so much to spread the word about mediumship. But it was fair to say that the majority of mediums took themselves very seriously indeed. They didn't do themselves any favours when it came to showing the world that psychics are, on the whole, ordinary people with extraordinary gifts. *Star Psychic* changed all that – it added a bit of fun and a bit of razzmatazz.

The series peaked at almost half a million viewers, which was impressive for a Freeview channel, and the bosses at ITV were overjoyed with the results. As I went back to work, clearing the 18-month backlog of clients that had grown while I was filming, early plans were being made for series two. But events conspired against me and the show was not recommissioned. Though hugely disappointed, I could understand why. Television stations were making budgetary cuts and the dark clouds of economic gloom were brewing on the horizon. Businesses were cutting back on advertising and with more and more channels springing up, the diminishing pot of advertising revenue on which ITV previously had a near monopoly was being stretched thinner and thinner. The result was that television companies had to think longer and harder about the type of programme they made and how much they spent. Now the accountants had more control than the programme makers. Still, I was assured that ITV wanted to use me in other shows and they began to look at different ideas for programmes I could front. One idea they came up with was a sort of psychic *Antiques Roadshow*, in which I would drive around the country in an old car, stopping off in towns and villages to look at people's knick-knacks and deliver readings based on the energy I picked up from them.

That idea never got off the ground and while discussions continued on how to use me and my unique skills, I busied myself back at home doing readings for my clients while I planned my next move.

It didn't occur to me straight away that there was any other way of sharing my gift with a larger audience. Without a television show I extended the opening hours of my practice and saw more people. And there were plenty more to see. There was a constant procession of clients trudging up the gravel drive of our three-bed semi in southwest London, not all of them pleased by my newfound fame. In fact the reaction from several long-standing clients was not favourable. Two of them in particular were concerned that my public profile would somehow affect them. One lady was one half of a very high-profile marriage and came to visit me weekly. Her husband was a well-known, powerful and well-connected personality. He was also controlling and insanely jealous and she was terrified he would find out about us and go crazy that she was telling someone like me all the secrets of their relationship. I had picked up a lot of incriminating information about him in the readings I did for her over the years and although I was incredibly discreet about our relationship, she feared that someone would find out she was seeing me.

She called me after the first *Star Psychic* was shown.

'Sally, I can't see you anymore,' she told me nervously. 'If he ever finds out there's no telling what he would do to me or you.'

I reassured her that I would never do anything to

jeopardise our arrangement or her privacy and discretion was always, and always would be, my main priority but I understood her decision and wished her love and happiness.

The other client who showed particular concern was also the wife of a well-known man. From the political classes, she was amazingly well connected. Each week she arrived in a chauffeur-driven government car and her driver parked round the corner. She would walk all the way down the crescent where I lived and kept her head down or wore a scarf so she wouldn't be recognised. We were on first name terms and she'd often call out of hours to speak to me. She too stopped seeing me. She explained in a phone call that she couldn't run the risk of being seen to be using the services of a medium.

Other high-profile clients were more open to the idea of seeing a celebrity psychic. One lady in particular was a public figure. She had married into an extremely rich family and was very supportive.

'This is great for you, Sally,' she told me when we met after the first show had been broadcast. 'Everything will happen for you now, your life will change.'

My life was indeed changing, but I was unsure of the direction it was taking. It was obvious that a new TV show was not going to happen overnight so I started to think about what else I could do and how I could carry on the momentum *Star Psychic* had created. I began to formulate an idea.

In the past I had attended spiritualist meetings and I had been to see John Edwards, another psychic, perform a stage show. Now I love John but the show I saw him do felt predictable. It was what I expected to see. There was no fanfare, no entertainment... like the spiritualist meetings I went to when I was young, it was a bit moody and serious. Given how well *Star Psychic* had been received, I started to wonder whether I could produce a stage version. And the more I considered it, the more it seemed like a good idea.

After several weeks of mulling it over I made one of the biggest decisions of my life: I told John to stop taking any new bookings because I was going on stage. I'd been talking to him about it for weeks and in principle he thought it was a good idea but that was before he realised just how serious I was. I broke the news over dinner one Thursday night. I'd just had a full day of clients and I was exhausted.

'How's your Chicken Kiev?' I asked idly to assess his mood.

'Fine, thanks,' he answered.

'I'm knackered,' I said.

'I'm not surprised. You've had a busy week,' he noted.

'Every week is busy,' I nodded. As the weeks went on I'd been feeling increasingly tired. More worryingly, I had also started feeling twinges in my chest, which I put down to overwork.

'I think it's time to stop taking bookings,' I blurted out.

At this John frowned.

'Do you need a holiday? We can afford one,' he offered.

'No, I'm giving up the practice for good. It's time we got this idea for the theatre show off the ground,' I said.

John nearly choked on a button mushroom. I was pulling the security blanket out from underneath us.

'But...' he spluttered.

I'm sure at that point my husband had a flashback to the day several decades before when I returned home from my safe and secure job as a dental nurse to announce that I was giving it all up to become a professional medium. His reaction then was: 'Are you off your trolley?' Now it was more muted. He stared at me while he turned it over in his head but he knew me well enough to realise that once I'd made up my mind, it was hard to stop me from doing what I intended to do.

And I knew I was doing the right thing; I trusted my intuition, which told me that it was time to move on and to make changes in my life. I could sense there were new things, bigger challenges and rewards over the horizon. I didn't worry that I'd never been on stage before and it didn't bother me. In the past I'd carried out readings in halls to around 50 people. I was confident that I could make a *Star Psychic* stage show work.

Over the following days John came round to the idea and we started planning. We stopped taking new bookings. I still had a large backlog of clients booked in to clear and would have to carry on doing readings even while I was touring but now I started to think about how the stage show would work. I definitely didn't want it to be like any other show out there – I wanted excitement, fun and pizzazz.

I had plans, I had definite ideas. I didn't know how they would evolve but I knew what I wanted: I wanted to develop the next generation of psychic shows. It was about time they were dragged into the 21st century. Usually there would be no music. Someone would walk on and introduce the act and the medium would walk out and start doing readings. It was formulaic and flat. I wanted to set the scene. I'd been to the theatre enough times to know that when the lights go down there's an atmosphere of excitement and expectation. There's an energy in the room and if I could harness that energy, I could create a great show. I wanted music, I wanted a montage, I wanted a big entrance and I wanted outfits… lots of them!

Over the next few months I managed to find a designer and a team who could put together what I wanted. I explained some of my ideas to the production manager.

'When I come out in the second half I want a costume change.'

'Why?' he frowned.

'If I was at the theatre watching a one-woman show, I would be wondering what she was going to wear. It's all part of the experience. Those are the kind of things us women think about,' I explained.

Given the fact that at the time I was around a size 26, it was hard enough finding one top to fit me, let alone two! Eventually I found a designer called Anna Scholtz, who makes clothes for large people in wonderful fabrics. I located all her stockists and bought tops from the range. It was a busy period and I was getting bigger. In the end I had to have my clothes made. I didn't realise then there were problems on the horizon – I actually felt healthier because I was up and moving around and because of that I wanted to *be* healthier. I wanted to get out and do things but my body was pulling me back. The twinges in my chest were increasingly common. Every now and then I would get sharp pains. My blood pressure was also high. But I ignored the warning signs and ploughed on.

There were several considerations we needed to take into account in order to stage a theatre production. In the TV show we used to have to run a legal disclaimer to point out that what viewers were seeing was for entertainment purposes only and we realised we would have to do the same thing with the theatre show so we made a voice-over to run at the start of the performance. The narrator explained that while my gift has not been scientifically proven, it has not been scientifically disproved either. All stage mediums had to run something similar.

I wanted people to leave letters and photos for

me so I could pick up messages from them. During the two hours that I would be on stage I was eager to reach out to as many people as I could and these 'love letters' would give me an ideal opportunity to include members of the audience in the proceedings. I realised it wouldn't be practical to hand everything back at the end of the night and I knew immediately that we had to treat these souvenirs with the utmost respect.

John and I sat down one night to decide what to do. Many of the photos left would be incredibly sentimental.

'How about if we create a memorial garden with them?' I proposed. 'We could burn them and put the ashes in the compost and then plant a rose garden using the compost.'

All my life I have loved roses. Wherever we have lived, I have always had roses. Even in our first house, where all we had was a yard, I had a bed cut and grew climbing roses there.

It seemed like the perfect idea and so that was what we did and continued to do over the years. John was a keen gardener and he was in charge of all the letters and photos. Eventually we had four massive compost bins where all the ashes went and 42 rose plants. John applied the compost twice a year and as the tour grew, people who didn't even come to the shows sent in photos to my office and asked for me to put them in the rose garden. I didn't dare tell the council in case they decided to designate my garden a memorial site.

Meanwhile, our plans for the tour took shape and we started to book venues. Theatres were open to the idea of hosting us, thanks to the exposure I'd enjoyed on the nation's television. Initially we had 60 dates booked for 2008 but we scaled that down to 30 as I was unsure whether the shows would work. Tickets were selling out… Then I started to get really nervous.

Psychic Sally was going on the road.

Chapter 3
A weighty matter

At this point in the story that there was an elephant in the room and that elephant was me because I was HUGE! By that stage in my life I was hovering around 20 stone. Morbidly obese, I was dealing with a range of health problems because of it.

My heart was struggling to cope, I had high blood pressure and was on medication to control it. I had regular oedema too – a condition where my legs and feet would swell so much I couldn't wear flip-flops or sandals. Flying was a nightmare because of the risk of deep vein thrombosis (DVT), which I developed one year and needed treatment for. Whenever I got a cold it inevitably developed into a chest infection and often progressed to agonising pneumonia. In early 2004 I suffered a particularly painful bout of infection and ended up in hospital after collapsing in the kitchen. I'd woken in agony and struggled downstairs in the middle of the night. I remember vividly standing hunched over in the kitchen, clinging to the work surface for support, with the moonlight filtering through the skylights. Terrified, I was coughing and wheezing, all the while praying for the pain to pass. Then I collapsed on my knees, all 20 stone of me. I'm lucky I didn't break something. I couldn't get back up and so I crawled to the phone and called for an ambulance. I ended up in Kingston Hospital.

For years I'd been yo-yo dieting. I'd go through phases where I would eat healthily and lose a few stone but then I'd start gorging on things like cake and biscuits and put the weight back on, plus a few extra pounds on top. My GP became so concerned about my weight that in 2004 he referred me to a specialist NHS clinic based in University College Hospital in London, where I met Professor Alberic Fiennes, one of the country's top bariatric surgeons. He was an expert in gastric bypass surgery.

Initially I was told a range of weight-loss surgery options were available. Bariatric surgery can either be restrictive, appetite suppressant, malabsorptive or a combination of all three. The common restrictive measure is to fit a band around the stomach. This technique is reversible; the band can be removed. The common appetite-suppressant method is the bypass, which works by re-routing part of the digestive system. This has the effect of profoundly reducing the appetite. Using keyhole surgery, surgeons re-plumb your digestive system in a number of ways and create a smaller stomach. Patients feel fuller faster and the process also limits the amount of fat the body can absorb. No quick fix, this is much bigger procedure and it is permanent. The surgery is major and afterwards life changes drastically as your body relearns what foods it can and cannot tolerate.

By the time I first met Alberic I had done my

homework on the Internet and I was aware of the implications. I'd researched the options and initially thought that a gastric band would be best for me.

'Simple,' I thought. 'Have it fitted for a while, lose the weight and then have it removed.'

As part of the process I was told to keep a food diary and diligently jotted down everything I ate over a two-week period. Reading it back was a sobering experience:

> *Monday breakfast: 3 croissants, tea, toast and marmalade. Snack: cake and a banana. Lunch: cheese sandwiches, crisps, cola, apple. Mid-afternoon snack: toast and pâté. Dinner: roast chicken, roast potatoes, veg, ice cream, tea and biscuits. Supper: cheese and biscuits.*

I was consuming 3,000 calories a day – in order to maintain a healthy weight I should have been eating around 1,800.

Alberic took one look at my food diary and told me I would need a bypass.

'I could fit a band and it might last a year or two but eventually you will have to have a bypass,' he explained. 'The problem is the type of foods you are prone to. Things like pâté and ice cream will pass through a band. If you were 30 and the weight you are now, maybe we could fit one and see how you get on for a few years but you are in your late-fifties now and you need something that will work and will allow you to enjoy your life.'

In the beginning my family were against the idea. Not because they didn't want to see me healthy again but because they were scared I'd flatline on the operating table. Gradually my loved ones came round to my way of thinking and realised that I would not have been referred for such serious surgery if an easier option were available, though.

So I went on the NHS waiting list for a gastric bypass. It was a long process that lasted three years and culminated around the time *Star Psychic* was on the television. All the time I was filming, I was preparing myself for surgery. I needed psychological evaluation to make sure I was mentally ready for the op and also to get to the root of my food addiction and make sure I understood the consequences of what I was going to have done. I had to be monitored regularly and I went on a special liver-reducing diet to lower my weight and ensure I was fit enough for the surgery, which involved a lot of very low fat food and small portions.

Because the show gave me exposure in the media I started to notice subtle ways in which the newspapers and magazines that wrote about me addressed my size. I was 'bubbly Sally Morgan' or 'larger than life Psychic Sally'. They were skilful adjectives used to convey the message that unlike most of the women on TV, I was fat. The funny thing was, apart from the effect it had on my health, my size never really bothered me. I didn't look in the mirror and weep; I wasn't vain, I just wanted to be more mobile and healthy.

The weight-loss practice I attended was based at the back of the hospital, away from the hustle and bustle of the main building. I used to say it was because society was ashamed of us – the morbidly obese patients, the ones who couldn't help themselves, the grossly overweight. We were ushered out the back, where we could be dealt with quietly, away from the more deserving patients. We'd all sit squeezed into the seats in the waiting room, trying not to make eye contact. We all knew why we were there; it was like Overeaters Anonymous.

By September 2007, when I was planning my stage show and waiting to see what other TV opportunities would come my way, I was ready and raring to go. The operation was booked for October and I had completed nearly three years of tests and evaluations. There were just a few final formalities to overcome, or so I thought. The pre-op heart and blood tests would finally verify that I was fit and well enough to go under the knife.

In any operation there is always a risk that something will happen when the patient is under general anaesthetic and with obese patients that risk is amplified. To make sure everything would be safe, I had been on medication to control my blood pressure and had undergone a gruelling diet (which consisted mainly of watery soup) to reduce the size of my liver so that when the surgeons performed the keyhole surgery they would have plenty of space to move around inside me.

The day after my 56th birthday I was due to have

my final cardiac check-up. The previous evening I had attended an ITV autumn ball held by Michael Grade, executive chairman of the TV broadcaster attended by many of the stars of the channel's shows and the producers and directors who made the programmes. Usually John would drive me up to the hospital and wait for me while I saw whatever specialist I was due to see but it was such a lovely warm late summer's afternoon and he was happily doing some gardening so it didn't seem fair to drag him out. Instead I decided to get the train on my own. Leaving my husband to have a rare few hours on his own to relax, I kissed him goodbye, walked to the railway station near our house and hopped on a train.

The journey was uneventful, if a little hot and sticky. On arrival the hospital cardiac unit was an air-conditioned haven away from the mad rush outside. London is always so full of people and traffic and on a hot day it can be a struggle just getting from A to B. I was glad to be in the relative calm of the cardiac unit and was ushered into an examination room once I'd checked in at reception. After a short wait a nurse came in, wheeling a big electrocardiogram machine, which would be used to monitor the activity in my heart. It had electrodes connected to wires hanging from it and dials and displays on the front panel.

'Please take off your top and bra, Mrs Morgan,' said the nurse kindly. 'I'm going to attach these pads to your body and monitor you for a while to get an idea of how well your heart is functioning.'

I've never particularly enjoyed undressing in front of strangers – who does? And so, awkwardly, I undressed and sat there, feeling embarrassed and exposed, trying my best to cover my ample boobs as the nurse busied herself with the machine. As she turned around to look at me with two wires in her hands, I saw a sudden flicker of recognition cross her face.

'Oh no,' I thought, 'she knows who I am!'

She smiled and reached out to start sticking plasters and wires around my boobs and asked sheepishly: 'I hope you don't mind me asking, but are you Sally Morgan from off the telly?'

'Yep, that's me,' I said, mortified. I'd never had a fan recognise me while I was naked before.

'Oh my God,' she said, 'wait till my family hear I've met *the* Sally Morgan!'

She was obviously too excited to think about patient confidentiality.

'And wait till you tell them you've touched her boobs,' I thought to myself.

Introductions over, she flicked on the machine and started looking at the readings that were spilling out of it on a long piece of paper. After a few minutes I saw a frown cloud her face.

'That's funny,' she muttered to herself, 'it was working earlier.'

After another few minutes checking and rechecking the machine she explained that it didn't appear to be working properly and she would have to go and get another. She left the room and then came back, wheeling a new machine. Once again I was hooked up and once again the machine began to spew out a paper record of my heart activity. This time the frown on her face was replaced by a look of concern.

'Is everything alright, love?' I asked.

'Erm, I'm not sure,' she stuttered. Then she added casually: 'Have you ever had heart problems before?'

I started to worry. 'What is it, nurse?' I said, shakily.

'Please don't get upset, Mrs Morgan,' she replied, 'I need to go and get a doctor. Just relax and I'll be back in a minute.'

Almost immediately she returned with two doctors, who came in with another machine and hooked me up to that as well. Once again the printout started to unfold. The doctors studied it intensely and quietly conferred. Finally, one of them turned to me and said: 'Mrs Morgan, I think you are having a heart attack.'

Chapter 4
Heart to heart

At first, the words did not register.

'Sorry, can you repeat that,' I said.

'Do not panic and try to relax,' he told me.

'Oh yeah,' I thought, 'that's easy for you to say, you're not the one having the heart attack.'

I could feel my heart racing and I was getting light-headed but I didn't know whether that was because I was going into cardiac arrest or because I was having a panic attack.

The doctor spoke calmly. 'It appears you are having a very mild heart attack. The readouts show that your heart is pumping abnormally. We need to get you to A&E and to monitor you.'

I was flabbergasted. It was like being slapped in the face. I couldn't quite believe what they were saying; I had genuinely felt fine. I wasn't in pain and the only thing that was hurting was my pride after so many people had been poking around at my boobs.

Like most people I always assumed having a heart attack would be an agonising experience. I wasn't doubled over in pain, clutching my chest. The worst I had felt over the last hour or so since I left the house was a little hot on the train and a bit breathless walking to the hospital. How could this be happening?

After that it was like a scene from *Casualty*. I slipped on my top but was still wired up to the machine and was put on a gurney and wheeled through to A&E, where I could be assessed and admitted, if need be. I kept on repeating, 'Honestly I'm fine, I'm not having a heart attack', but the experts knew better. I was rushed through corridors with my top flapping open. When I got to A&E, another nurse recognised me and directed me to a quiet, secluded examination room.

Another specialist came in and, despite my protestations, reconfirmed that I was having a mild heart attack.

'But I feel fine,' I insisted. 'I just need to go home and have a sit down.'

Then she said something I've never forgotten.

'Mrs Morgan, how many eyes have you got?'

'Two, of course,' I answered.

'And how many kidneys have you got?'

'Two… why are you asking these questions?' I thought maybe it was a test to make sure I was fully conscious and lucid.

'And how many hearts do you have?'

Then it hit me.

'Just the one,' I sighed.

If that was broken there was nothing to take its place.

'You are staying here, you are not going anywhere and we are going to take care of you,' the doctor soothed.

I'll never forget that conversation. It brought

everything into focus. For years before I decided to have gastric surgery I had kidded myself that the illnesses I was prone to could be cleared up with medicine and life could then carry on normally. I had blocked out the bigger picture and tried to ignore the permanent damage I was quite obviously doing to myself. But now all those years of what was tantamount to self-abuse had come home to roost. My heart, a vital organ, was damaged.

I was assessed and taken to a cardiac care unit, where I was put on drips to feed me medication that would stabilise my heart. Then I was wired up to more machines to monitor my breathing, blood oxygen levels and heart activity.

'Please, you need to call my husband and tell him what has happened,' I begged the staff.

John got the most terrifying phone call of his life. He later told me that as he raced up to the hospital to be with me he didn't know whether I would be alive or dead when he reached me. The hospital had told him what had happened and that he needed to come as soon as he could.

On arrival he had to choke back the tears at seeing me lying prone and pale, wired up to machines and visibly shaken. He stroked my hand and reassured me that everything would be OK. The doctors increased my blood pressure pills and put me on a strong diuretic. After a few days, when the danger had passed and the medication had begun to work, I was released but then had to book in to see a consultant cardiologist so that I could undergo a series of other tests to find what was wrong and ultimately get my heart healthy again.

I should have been counting my lucky stars that the problem was discovered before I underwent the gastric bypass op. Without that minor heart attack there was a strong chance I would have suffered a major one on the operating table and that could well have proved fatal. In a way, that heart attack saved my life but at the time I didn't feel thankful at all because it meant that the surgery I had been looking forward to for so long and had been working so hard towards now had to be cancelled. In fact, all the way through the ordeal that thought was at the back of my mind: no more op. The light at the end of the tunnel that I had been working towards for so long went out and all I felt was a crushing disappointment.

Over the following weeks the knowledge that I had come close to such a serious problem really started to sink in. I knew I was ill, I knew my heart was suffering from the strain I was putting on it. On my first appointment with the cardiologist after the heart attack I walked into his office and begged him: 'I still want this operation, I still need to have the gastric surgery. When can I have it?'

He was encouraging and told me: 'Sally, you *will* have it. We want you to have it too and you need to have it. You wouldn't be here if you didn't need it but first we need to get you better.'

Later I spoke to my surgeon Alberic Fiennes,

who was wonderfully sympathetic but concurred with the cardiologist and confirmed that I needed to sort my heart out first before he would consider performing the operation on me. So I went from the top of the NHS waiting list to the bottom again.

Over the following months I had regular check-ups at the cardiac unit in University College Hospital. In fact I had a barrage of tests. During one of the most unpleasant ones a drip was put in my arm and I was administered a drug that made my heart race faster and faster. Lying on my side I thought my chest was going to burst. It's hard to explain the feeling but it was like running a marathon while you are lying down. I could feel my heart pounding through my ribcage and I was breathless and sweaty, but I was dead still on a bed in a quiet room. It's not an experience I would recommend to anyone. They discovered one of the walls of my heart was thickening – a conse-quence of high blood pressure. I was also told I was just weeks away from becoming diabetic and prescribed yet more tablets, which included statins to lower the high levels of cholesterol in my blood.

I'd been so scared by what happened that I put myself on a low-fat diet, cutting out breads and starchy carbohydrates and lost another two stone in three months. At a further check-up the cardiologist told me: 'That's fantastic, Sally! You keep this up and you'll be ready for the operation again soon.'

But the months went on. The damage I had done

to my heart was not going to heal itself overnight. Eventually, in November 2007, I was discharged as an outpatient from the cardiac unit and left my last appointment with mixed feelings. Of course I was happy that the immediate danger had passed and my condition had stabilised, even though I would still have to have regular check-ups with my GP. However, in terms of the gastric surgery, I would need to start at the beginning again. It had been so traumatic I decided to put my operation plans on ice for a while and see how I felt after a few months. And as the weeks passed I felt less and less inclined to begin the whole process again. There were so many opportunities coming my way and I couldn't see where I would find the time or the mental space to concentrate on such a major task. Professionally, I wanted to make hay while the sun was shining.

I wondered if being thinner would help my TV career and if being obese was holding me back. After all, television has the reputation of being an image-obsessed industry and being on-screen adds around 10lbs to your appearance. I think maybe my size did work against me initially. I'd been a high-profile psychic for many years and had built up that profile and fanbase through hard work, word of mouth and magazine and newspaper articles before anyone decided to take a chance and give me my own television show. Maybe if I were thinner things would have happened for me sooner, but as *Star Psychic* came to an end my size became part of my persona and many fans found it inspiring. After all, if a morbidly obese woman can find fame and fortune on TV in her fifties, there is hope for us all!

Chapter 5
On the road

The posters made it all seem real: 'An Audience with Sally Morgan; straight from her successful TV series'. I was actually going to do it! I was going on tour. Excited and nervous in equal measure, I had sensed that a change was coming and it had finally arrived. But I still had a few client commitments so I planned to start small.

Although I had no idea how I would be received and whether the concept would work, I wasn't worried about connecting with spirit; that was the one thing I knew and trusted would be success-ful. The nerves were financial ones. I was taking a giant leap into the world of theatre. My practice at home was running comfortably and I had plenty of work. What if it didn't work out? What if no one came to see me and the shows were a flop? What if I was rubbish? I had a feeling everything would work out, but as with most things in my life, I was unable and unwilling to turn my psychic gift on myself and predict my own future. It never worked that way. Believe me, I'd tried. On occasion I had tried to visualise the winning lottery numbers and conjure up the name of the winning horse at the Grand National. Who wouldn't? But every time I asked spirit for a clue all I got was silence. The gift

I had been given came with a set of restrictions: it was to be used only to help others. So I faced the new chapter of my life with a mix of confidence and apprehension.

'Are we doing the right thing, John?' I asked, one night a few weeks before the first date.

'It's too late to back down now,' he shrugged.

Then he reassured me that if it didn't work out I could always go back to doing readings from home. Initially that was the plan: I would do the tour and then resume where I had left off. We had a Plan B.

As the first date grew nearer I began to think about how I would act on stage. I didn't rehearse because I didn't feel the need to – I believed that as a medium you must act as truthfully as possible. The minute you start dressing up what you do, you begin to lose authenticity. I had been myself on the TV show and I wanted to be myself on the stage too. Personally, I could only receive messages by being true to myself and acting genuinely. I knew that if I started embellishing my act with mumbo jumbo and mysticism I'd lose respect for myself and from spirit. They come to me because I'm me, if I tried to be someone else it just wouldn't work.

I had no stage training but I'd always known from an early age that I would become famous and so in a funny way I was prepared for it. One of my earliest memories was of being a little girl in the house where I grew up in Fulham. I was sitting at my mum's dressing table, looking at myself in the mirror and singing into Mum's hairbrush as if it were a microphone. The house was haunted and the spirit of one particular man would often show himself. He was a very tall black man with a large Afro hairstyle. Back in those days there wasn't the multicultural mix there is in London today and it was very unusual to see anyone who wasn't white. I saw the man's reflection in the mirror. His head was peeking round the door behind me and he watched me intently as I sang. When I turned round to look, there was no one there. I stopped singing and went to find Mum, who was in the kitchen downstairs.

I told her what had happened.

'You'll see the Devil in the mirror,' she half-joked. 'Anyway, what were you doing, singing in my bedroom? You're always singing and pretending you are a pop star.'

'I'm going to be famous one day,' I replied. And I really believed it. To me it seemed obvious and so as the day arrived for my first theatre show I felt that I was heading for my natural environment to fulfil my destiny. Prior to that first tour the largest audience I'd stood in front of was around 50. Occasionally I did demonstrations in village halls or community centres but I'd never stepped out in front of an auditorium audience before. I wasn't nervous, though – I was so caught up in the buzz around *Star Psychic* I thought I was invincible. And I was convinced I had the Midas touch and everything I touched would turn to theatrical gold, I'll admit it, I believed my own hype. Besides, money was not the motivation for the tour – I wanted to get to more people. I wanted to show the world the wonderful things that happened when you put your trust in the spirit world. People had been given a flavour of the power of spirit through the television show and I believed that theatre shows would allow them to witness psychic happenings in person.

The tour started in the autumn of 2008, around the same time *Star Psychic* was repeated on TV, which was an unplanned bonus. In all it had taken about a year to organise and while it was being planned, I cleared most of the backlog of people who had booked in to see me at my home.

The first date was at a theatre in Billingham, County Durham. John drove me up there and we spent most of the day in the car. Throughout the journey I couldn't stop talking about what an amazing show it was going to be. It was my debut and I was playing the same 500-seater venue for two nights because tickets had sold so well.

I had arranged a treat for the audience. One of the most popular parts of *Star Psychic* was the celebrity reading and I thought it would be a good idea to have a celebrity guest with me on stage so I invited Darryn Lyons, the paparazzi photographer who had become a TV personality. He was going to come on stage and I'd talk to him about the reading I had given him in the TV show. I thought it would be riveting.

By the time the curtain went up I was buzzing, and not just with excitement. There was something happening in my mind that I didn't quite understand. Something had been building within me all day. It's hard to explain but it was an energy. It didn't feel painful or unpleasant and when I eventually stepped out into the spotlight I felt it surge through me. I don't take drugs and I never have but I imagine it may have been like the feeling people get when they take cocaine – the surge of energy was accompanied by a barrage of images, sounds and thoughts. They were not my own. It felt like someone was fast-forwarding a video in my head. There were scenes flashing through my mind. Spirit was bombarding me and so I concentrated hard on channelling what I was seeing, feeling and thinking.

Somehow I managed to get a grip on the strange process that was happening in my mind. I knew it was my psychic antennae going into overdrive. It was the same process I had experienced when I read for individuals but this time it was turbocharged beyond anything I had known before.

The show began and I started deciphering what I was feeling. And the hits came; spirit didn't let me down. It was strange being up on that stage in front of 500 people but I loved it. Looking back, I was probably terrible. There were elements of the show that worked and some that didn't. When I introduced Darryn the energy I had felt and that had been building throughout the show seemed to subside. People switched off and started talking amongst themselves.

'Who's he?' someone called out.

'Get him off!' shouted someone else.

In my modesty I hadn't realised that they had come to see me and to receive messages. All the time I was faffing around with Darryn, the audience was being left out. I didn't know what I was doing.

'Get on with it!' another woman called out.

Then a woman behind her grabbed her.

''Ere, you leave Sally alone!' she said.

The women started arguing and the argument broke out into a fight. Someone picked up a bottle and threw it; fists flew, hair was yanked. The bouncers came in and broke it up. Shell-shocked, I stood on stage and watched the drama unfold until I saw one of the crew ducking in the wings and beckoning me to come off stage for my own safety. It was like a scene from a cowboy movie.

When things had calmed down the show resumed. Afterwards I spoke to the theatre manager.

'What happened there?' I asked. 'It was terrifying.'

He shrugged.

'What do you expect, love? It's Friday night, everyone is drunk. Friday night is fight night!'

It took a while for my ego to accept that there was one extra dead person on stage that night: me. In theatrical terms I'd died and no amount of psychic energy was going to save me. At the time I thought that inaugural show had been amazing.

For me the first dates were a real learning curve but despite this I knew in those shambolic days I was meant to stand on stage and be the type of medium who shared her ability with large crowds. It was all about the energy and the effect it had on the combined mass of people and me.

So I honed what people in theatre call my stage-craft. Soon I got used to addressing large groups of people but I always stayed true to myself – I never acted, there were no rehearsals. Before each show I did a soundcheck and a walk-on, which is where the stage manager came to my dressing room before the show at about 5pm and took me on the route I needed to take to get to the edge of the stage. I was shown the hold line, which is the location you stand in behind the curtain, where the audience can't see you. Then I would walk out onto the stage and look out at the empty theatre. It used to take my breath away, thinking that in a matter of hours all those seats would be full.

Sometimes I'd get nervous and the production manager would lie to me and tell me the theatre would be only half-full because not many people had bought tickets. I would be relieved, believing I'd only be playing to a small number of people. By the time I walked on and realised he'd lied it was too late and I would inevitably come off stage at the end of the show and call him something unprintable.

At each show I tried my best to get messages to as many people as possible. I was manic and after each performance I struggled with the knowledge that inevitably there were those who went away disappointed. There were so many who turned up to see me in the hope that they would get messages from loved ones, it wasn't possible to give them all what they wanted. I tried so hard to please everyone. I remember walking off one night thinking, 'I don't know if I want to do this, I am making myself ill because I want to please them all.' In the end my production manager told me I needed to slow down and concentrate on quality rather than quantity.

We worked out a routine. John would drive me to the venues and I would drive home because he can't see in the dark. He can't see in the rain either and he really doesn't like the sun in his eyes so we were OK as long as it was lightly overcast!

The shows were all over the country and we would stay in really grotty hotels to save money. After each show I would be exhausted and the only thing that kept me going was food because it gave me energy. We would have a stock of Marks & Spencer sandwiches for the way home and so I drove and ate, and just got bigger and bigger.

Sadly, you can't eat properly when you spend a lot of time travelling on the UK's motorways. After some gigs the first thing we did was track down the nearest fish and chip shop because the more calorific the food, the more awake I felt. Despite my recent health scare I still enjoyed food and eating and it was a great comfort for me after the mental strain of being up on stage to gorge myself on junk food. I didn't realise the problems that were on the horizon – I actually felt healthier because I was up and moving around.

I measured my success by the reaction I got at each show. Now I was living day by day, which was such a new concept. It was a ride, completely uncharted territory, and we were all watching to see what would happen. None of us knew where it would lead. Those were exciting times. I didn't miss home because I was loving the whole novelty of it all. After all, I'd been shut in my little office at home for so many years it was like a breath of fresh air and anything was possible.

Around that time I was asked to do a private job for a client and although I had stopped taking bookings I could hardly refuse. That client was the singer-songwriter George Michael and I was asked to do readings at a birthday party his then partner Kenny Goss was holding for him at their beautiful riverside home in Oxford. I was asked to go there because the girl who was doing the flowers for the party was a friend of mine and she'd recommended me. Her name was Hayley and she owned a lovely florist's called Absolute Flowers.

It was a summer's evening and the grounds at the back of George's house were beautiful. The organisers had erected a series of Turkish-style tents and inside each one they had laid out magnificent ornate furniture. I was able to choose a tent in which to set up and throughout the evening a procession of famous people wandered in for readings. There were other people there too to entertain the guests. Next to my tent a lady was giving tarot readings.

At one stage, late in the night, two young girls walked in, accompanied by a man I immediately recognised as one of the Goss twins, who used to be in the band Bros. The girls looked to be in their mid-teens and they were done up to the nines. I had no idea who they were. They asked if I'd give them a reading and I automatically refused because I have strict rules about giving children readings.

The Goss chap spoke to me and told me that one of the girls were Bob Geldof's daughter, Peaches. I explained that it didn't matter who she was, I didn't think it was appropriate to read for youngsters. Indeed once I heard who she was I was even more cautious as I knew her mother's tragic history. Paula Yates, her mum, had died of an accidental heroin overdose when she was young. The girls, however, wouldn't take no for an answer and protested and pleaded. I asked if Peaches' father was with them and explained that if he wanted to sit in, I might talk to all three of them but they had lost interest by that point.

Several days later there was an article in a newspaper claiming I had done a reading for the Geldof girls, which was untrue and certainly did not come from me. I never talk to the press about the content of my readings, they remain a secret between me and the person I am reading for. Even though there are no rules that govern mediums I believe that you can't do the type of work I do without a strong set of ethics; you just have to work out those ethics yourself. I have my own set of rules that I stick to and one of those rules is that I don't give readings to children. And if that person is on the cusp of being an adult, as the Geldof girl was, I like a parent or adult to be there with them.

Chapter 6
Lost in theatreland

It was a real learning curve for me but I knew in those early days that I was meant to stand on stage and be the type of theatre medium who takes their gift to big audiences. It felt right. I've always trusted my intuition and it was telling me I was on the right path. I thought back to my childhood, to my insistence that I would be famous one day. From a young age I was taken to see shows. Panto was a family tradition and I loved the magical feeling as the house lights went down and the curtain came up.

'I'm going to be an actress,' I'd tell Mum.

I kept on and on at my mother about it until eventually she tried to get me into stage school. As luck would have it, she worked with a lady whose son is now a famous playwright: a man called Ronnie Harwood. After I'd nagged her constantly about being an actress Mum finally arranged a meeting with Ronnie. She took me to see him at his home in a smart part of London – I must have been only around 10 years old at the time. He'd made some lunch for us: fish paste and cucumber sandwiches. It all seemed so posh. After tea and sandwiches he took me to his study and he asked me why I wanted to be on stage.

'I want to be an actress,' I told him.

A little cockney sparrow, I wanted to fly. I had visions of myself on the West End stage, bowing to an appreciative audience. Mr Harwood must have seen a spark of something promising in me because after we'd chatted about theatre and my favourite shows he had a quiet word with my mum. He told her that I was too young but if I was still interested when I was 16, he would have a word with a few of his contacts and try and get me into a rep company he knew. Rep, or repertory theatre companies, was the testing ground for up-and-coming acting talent so Mr Harwood's offer might have been my route to fame and fortune but I never heard about it. I didn't know that he had offered to help me realise my dream until much later in life when Mum told me. Apparently after that meeting she went home and told Dad but he forbade it, adding there was to be no more mention of it. A working-class man to his roots, he believed in an honest day's work for an honest day's pay. He certainly didn't think prancing around on stage was a decent way to make a living. So I never did get the chance to try my hand out as an actress. Even now, I'd never say never – I'd love a part in one of the soaps, should the opportunity arise!

With my thespian ambitions thwarted before they even began, I eventually took to the stage at the grand old age of 57. And I made sure I milked the opportunity for all it was worth. According to the promoter at the time I 'took to the green' (the phrase theatre folk use to describe going on stage) as naturally as anyone he'd seen.

'You were meant to be on stage,' I was told.

I got some good write-ups in the local papers too because I was on the telly. If anyone thought I was going to disappear after *Star Psychic* and sneak back to my cosy life in suburbia they could think again – I was going to be big in theatreland!

I loved seeing my face on the posters outside the venues. Not because I was vain in any way. Heaven knows, I was a big girl. But those posters reminded me that I was doing the work I was destined to do and I enjoyed every show because I got to meet some amazing people and help those who needed reassurance. Both spiritually and physically, I made an effort. I tried to be as honest as possible too. When the hits started happening I was as surprised as the audience and it showed. I'd gasp when I got something spot-on and I'd laugh and cry with the people who took the messages: the receivers.

I believed that if someone had bought a ticket and spent their hard-earned cash on coming to see me, I owed it to them to make an effort. I wanted to look nice on stage too. Which left me in a bit of a quandary because for most of my adult life I had hardly ever worn make-up and suddenly I realised that you can't hide on stage when there are lights on you and a camera is beaming your image onto a big screen. If you don't wear a bit of slap and some lippy under those conditions it is very easy to look pale and drawn.

I had never worn foundation before I started touring. Even as a teenager and a young woman, while all my friends wore it, I never bothered. I might have put a bit of mascara on if I went out or applied some lipstick but apart from that, nothing. It was not unusual, I suppose. In the sixties when everyone was going in for huge lashes and kohl liner I went nude! I'm not sure why I was never a make-up lover. I tend to touch my face a lot and rub my eyes – I suppose I realised that if I did use it, I'd end up with it spread across my face. Plus, I never felt I needed it. There were times when I felt compelled to buy it and try it out again because that's what women did. John would always tell me I didn't need it but he wasn't being jealous or controlling, he was right. I was lucky; I had a clear, clean complexion and I didn't need it. But as soon as I began doing the shows without a face on, I realised I needed to start. One day I looked really tired and realised how much it was amplified on stage so I went out and bought myself some foundation.

It was a huge learning curve working out what to do with it but thankfully I'd started doing magazine shoots for publicity purposes and when you do photoshoots you are lucky enough to have a hair and make-up artist who applies the make-up and makes sure you look right. It was a luxury and I watched what they did carefully. They were real artists and with their powders and lotions they managed to make me look completely different. I'd buy similar products to what they used, although I always spent a little more as they tended to use the cheap stuff! And that's how I learnt to put on my stage face. I practised it so much over the years that before too long it took just ten minutes to do.

I was lucky enough to have a fantastic hairdresser, who I have known and used for many years. She became a personal friend. I loved her to bits and she came by royal appointment. Her name was Denise McAdam. She used to be the Princess of Wales' hairdresser and that was how I met her: it was 25 years ago at the Palace. I was there to see one of my clients who worked in the royal household and we got talking and got on like a house on fire. Denise has been doing my hair ever since. She did Sarah Ferguson's hair when she married Prince Andrew in 1986 and she cuts Prince Charles's hair too. The royal family call her 'Och Aye' because she's Scottish. They love her too and she was given the Royal Victorian Medal for hairdressing services to the royal family in 2010. So, in terms of hair, I had it covered!

Over the first tour the show evolved. Certain aspects were dropped and one of the first to go was the celebrity element. While *Star Psychic* had been very much about me interacting with other celebs, I soon realised that the stage show had to be about the audience and me and nothing else should get in the way.

The show was about readings and about displaying the amazing link I could make with the spirit world. It was all about the energy I could harness between the living and the dead. At that early point I hadn't worked it out. When I looked back later it frightened me to think how naive I was. The energy which came from spirit when a large group of people opened up and trusted in the possibility of an afterlife was immense. A complete novice I was there, juggling with it. I was used to sitting in a small room with one other person and suddenly I had plonked myself on stages up and down the UK and channelled what is the most primal and pure force in the natural world. For this I had no coaching because there were no rules; I used intuition and trust. I trusted spirit and had faith that what I was doing was for good, which it was. My intentions were and always had been pure: I wanted to help people. I didn't think too hard about what I was doing, which, with hindsight, is probably a good thing because had I done so I would probably have packed up. My gift was allowed to develop naturally; it evolved and the whole process was organic. I think that's why it worked – there were no airs and graces and it wasn't forced.

As I soon discovered there was a world of difference between the readings I had been giving at home and those I was now giving on stage. For a start the subject matter I was dealing with was head-spinning. There were so many spirits lining up to talk to their loved ones and each one had a different story. Every death is unique, like a fingerprint, and in a single night I found that I might be dealing with sickness, suicide, murder and accidents. And then there were the children. Of course I'd received messages from children in spirit before in the privacy of my office. At first I struggled with the idea of taking their messages in front of an audience; I wondered if it was right. But the children came through to me for a reason: they wanted to speak to their mummies and daddies so who was I to stop them? It was part of my duty to take those messages and relay them as truthfully and as accurately as I could.

One of those first messages still sticks in my memory:

'Mummy? Mummy? My neck hurts.'

I was on stage in a northern town. The auditorium became deadly silent as I repeated what I was sensing in my head. It's hard to explain what happens when messages come through. Although I often describe them as 'voices' –which makes me sound mad – they are more like thought patterns and the one I was sensing cut through all the other voices and thoughts that were swirling round in my head. It was a little girl. So I reached out and grabbed hold of the message as it twisted around in my head like someone would grab a loose balloon string on a windy day. I held it and pulled it towards me, pushing the other thoughts and visions to one side so that I could focus on it. It was very clear, not loud or panicky but puzzled. I tuned in on it as you would tune a radio in the days before push-button DAB. As I concentrated the image of a pretty little girl popped into my head. Immediately I knew her name was Emily. In the image she was holding her throat. Her face was red. I felt a strange sensation in my own throat, a constriction. Instinctively, I raised my hand to my neck, mirroring what I was seeing and feeling.

'I have a little girl here. She's five. Her name is Emily and she wants her Mummy,' I explained to the audience.

There was a shuffling somewhere at the back of the auditorium. More details dropped into my mind.

'I get the name Jane and I can see a slice of birthday cake,' I continued. Then I started coughing as the tightness in my throat intensified.

'I'm really having trouble breathing,' I said. 'I think this little girl choked on a piece of birthday cake.'

The pleas from the little girl were becoming more urgent.

As I looked over at the back of the theatre I saw a hand go up. A lady stood up from her seat, hesitant. As she did so the message became clearer. I took that as a sign that the message was meant for her.

'Are you this little girl's mum?' I asked gently.

The pressure in my throat eased as she nodded.

'I'm Jane,' she said. 'Emily is my daughter.'

'She's in spirit, isn't she?'

I knew the answer was yes.

The woman nodded. She blinked and tears dripped down her cheeks. The visions continued. I could see a birthday party and children singing 'Happy Birthday'. Candles were blown out. Then I started to feel hot and prickly. I explained all this to Jane and she nodded sadly.

'Emily had a nut allergy,' she told me. 'We didn't know how severe it was. She had cake at a party and she had an allergic reaction. She couldn't breathe. By the time the ambulance men arrived, she'd slipped into a coma. She never woke.'

As Jane explained the tragedy I was overcome by a feeling of warmth, love and utter contentment. Emily's spirit was drawing love from her, sucking up the maternal bond and reassuring me that she was at peace and in a beautiful place.

'Emily wants you to know she is in a wonderful place. She's in Heaven.'

I saw the image of a bedroom. It was a little girl's room decorated with Disney Princess wallpaper and strewn with Barbie dolls and soft toys. I described what I was seeing.

'That's her bedroom,' nodded Jane.

'Emily is there,' I explained. 'Whenever you need to feel her, go to the room and she'll be there with you. She loves you very much.'

'I love her very much too.' Jane was sobbing. 'Thank you, Sally, thank you *so* much.'

In the early days of my first tour readings such as these made me realise the weight of responsibility I was carrying. While there was as much light-hearted humour as there was sadness during the shows, I vowed to always be true and to pass on exactly what I was sensing as making the connection between the living and dead was profound for the receivers. In many cases it was life changing. After the shows I signed autographs; audience members would wait for me to come out and many of those who had taken messages would tell me that I had changed their lives and made them believe in the possibility of an afterlife. That's a major thing to be able to do and it wasn't, and never has been, something I take lightly.

During the shows I discovered I could sense spirit more. All my senses were far more heightened with a large group of people in front of me: I was supercharged! When a receiver stood and took a message I realised that I could tune in and push other messages to the side. It was a skill I found hard at first but the more I practised, the better I got. I juggled the messages. I also learnt that I could get more information when a receiver stood with another person. For some reason the information I picked up became clearer. It was like having a booster aerial or putting two plugs in an electrical point and getting twice the amount of juice.

All this took a bit of getting used to. It was like a cacophony of thoughts and feelings going off in my head. I wasn't an academic, I'm not clever, yet there was something amazing going on in my brain that was filtering an amazing amount of information in a way that was coherent and allowed me to verbalise what I was sensing and explain to the audience in a way that made sense. It really should have come out as mumbo jumbo but I seemed to have an ability to order it. There were plenty of times when the messages didn't make sense initially and many instances when I would be talking to a receiver and the details I was giving made no sense to them. It was only later the penny dropped and they realised that the details were relevant to them after all. Many people wrote to me after shows or waited for me at the stage door to explain that they had only realised the significance of some of the details I was passing on after their readings. Every message was an experiment, with no two the same. Like beautiful snowflakes, they were individual and fleeting. It was a privilege to be able to catch them before they melted back into the universe.

Once the messages had gone I knew I had to let them go. I couldn't bring them back and I couldn't take them on. While I was emotionally attached to the message and the receiver when I was acting as a conduit between this world and the spirit world, I knew that once that link had dissolved, I had to let go of the emotion that it carried. I couldn't burden myself with the grief and tragedy that the living carry for the dead, it would be too much to cope with and it would interfere with the clarity of the subsequent messages I gave.

I felt energised after each show. My adrenaline

levels peaked and you could have scraped me off the ceiling following those first appearances. Then, when it was all over and I was back at the hotel or in the car, I went very quiet: I buzzed inside but I didn't want to talk. The last thing I found I wanted to do was discuss it.

I discovered themes common to most of my shows. Suicide was one such recurring subject. It was a difficult one to tackle with an audience because it comes loaded with so many emotions: guilt, anger, shock and in some faiths even disgust, which is something that annoys me. As far as I'm concerned there is no shame in suicide. People who find themselves caught up in the tsunami of emotions that lead them to take their own lives are at peace in Heaven. I know – I speak to them regularly. Knowing this allowed me to give countless relatives and loved ones peace of mind.

At one show the image of a stool dropped into my mind. Spirit world and our world overlaid each other in front of me and I saw the stool there in front of me on the stage. I could only see the bottom half of it. Suddenly it rocked and fell over. I jumped. In my head I heard the clatter as it fell and I saw a pair of legs dangling above it. They kicked and jerked wildly, then tensed, shuddered and finally stopped. Then they hung there, slowly swaying to and fro. At this I swallowed; I knew exactly what I'd seen. I had witnessed the last moments of a man's life as he hung himself.

I picked up the name David.

'I have a David here,' I told the audience. 'He hung himself.'

There was no reaction from the crowd. I explained in detail what I'd seen. There was something puzzling me: in the majority of messages I received I saw a whole scene. The spirit delivering the message would show me how he or she looked so I could describe their appearance. David, however, was only showing me the bottom half of his legs, swinging silently above a wooden stool. Intuitively, I knew this was a salient point.

'I can only see the bottom half of this man's legs,' I explained.

The pieces of the puzzle dropped neatly into place with that bit of information and a hand was raised. A woman stood up.

'That's how we found him,' she told me. 'David was my son. He hung himself in the garage with the garage door half open. We returned home and from the driveway all we could see was the bottom of his legs.'

It was an amazingly accurate scene and once the lady had taken the message I was able to reassure her that her son was at peace and that he loved her.

Word was spreading about my uncanny ability to read from spirit. My A-list client base was expanding too. It's an area of my work that I remain guarded about. While touring I had many high-profile clients that I continued to see because I had a duty to them. Many of them had become friends. One gentleman who I saw regularly and who became a family friend was Mitch Winehouse, Amy's dad. Mitch is a lovely bloke. He's a down-to-earth cabbie and a hugely devoted father. I saw him while Amy was alive and he was worried sick – the poor girl was very mixed-up and had fallen in with the wrong crowd. Mitch did all he could to help her. I hope he gained some peace of mind from the sessions we shared.

I loved being able to help people come to terms with their grief – it felt purposeful. By now I was doing shows all over the UK. I had closed my practice to become a travelling medium and all my energies were focussed on the shows but I still didn't have a long-term plan and I was living day to day. It was such a new concept for me; it was a ride, it was so refreshing. Me and my family were all watching to see what would happen. It was completely uncharted territory and none of us knew where it was leading.

I didn't miss home because I loved the novelty of being out on the road. For so many years I had been shut in my little office that it was a breath of fresh air. I worked hard to make it a success. All my life I have carried a strong work ethic and it didn't let me rest on my laurels. I come from a working-class background and was taught that if you don't work, you don't get. And I was never allowed to shirk. When I was in my early twenties, living at home, my dad made sure I went to work. One day I remember waking up and feeling that I didn't want to go in. I was feeling under the weather, but

Dad came into my room, lifted my bed up from one end and tipped me unceremoniously out of the sheets I was wrapped in.

'Why aren't you up? You need to go to work,' he scolded.

'I don't want to go today,' I explained.

'Well, that's tough! You're going, you ain't sitting in here all day.'

I knew that if I insisted on staying he would just chuck me out of the house anyway so I got up, got myself dressed and went to work. There was never a time when I thought I couldn't go to work – I had a job and therefore I had a commitment, a duty and a loyalty not only to the people I had agreed to work for, but also to myself to earn money. I come from a family who have never claimed benefits. Even if they were down to nothing, they would still find a way to earn rather than look for handouts. My parents told me that there are always jobs out there – you clean toilets if you have to, but you work, end of story. So I couldn't ever imagine myself not working.

I've been accused of being a workaholic but I am just a person who thinks that if I want something in life I have to earn the money for it and for that reason I continued to tour. And once that first tour was over I went straight back to doing a few readings from home while arrangements were made to book more venues and start another year of live shows. There was a demand for my work: people believed in me and they wanted to see me. As long as that demand was there, I would carry on touring.

Chapter 7
Wedding belles

I love opportunity. I don't believe you should ever give up looking for it or that you should turn it down without a very good reason so when I was contacted by a publisher in 2008 and asked to write my life story I leapt at the chance. Initially I thought, 'Why would anyone be interested in me and my life?' but the publisher reassured me.

'People are fascinated by you and what you do,' they explained. 'It's your chance to tell your story in your words.'

I was helped and guided through the process but I had strong opinions about what I wanted to include in the book. I wanted to let people know what it's like to be psychic, what my childhood was like, who my family were and how I became a professional medium. The publisher asked if I would talk about my famous clients, specifically about Diana, Princess of Wales. I thought long and hard about that one. While it was public knowledge through no fault of my own that Diana had been a client of mine, I had never betrayed her trust and given away details of our conversations; I was adamant that I never would. So I wrote generally about our relationship without divulging the often-shocking details of the conversations we had. And no, I'm not going to break that rule and spill the royal beans here!

I found the process of writing my life story fascinating. It made me think long and hard about my life for the first time. From the beginning to the present I had to remember all the important things that had happened and think about why they happened; why I did what I did. Under normal circumstances you don't evaluate your life chronologically in such a way. You don't sit down for months on end and think about what you did as a child, how you were treated or about the people in your life. I found the best way to deal with it was to imagine my life as a journey across a river along a set of stepping-stones. Each stone was an important event in my life that led to the next. I plotted my journey through life in this way and along the route I started to learn things about myself. It was like going through therapy; I analysed everything.

It was hard sometimes. I had to revisit difficult areas of my life, particularly my estranged relationship with my eldest daughter, Jemma. I do not talk about details of what happened and she is always in my heart. There isn't a day that goes by when she's not in my thoughts. I realised how, at certain parts of my life, I was closely linked to loss and how that had impacted on my work over the years. I understand loss and because of what happened with my daughter I know what it means to lose someone. My work is all about loss and because of that occasionally my own loss comes into focus. It forms the basis of the empathy I have with those for whom I do readings. I've always believed that to do what I do at the level I do it you need to understand in part what the people you read for are going through and having lost a child, which in effect I have, helps me understand some of the pain I come into contact with. For me the only difference is that perhaps there is a glimmer of hope that one day in this life I might be reconciled in some way with the loved one I have lost. That's not an option for those I see whose loved ones have passed into spirit; their loss lasts until they are reunited. I have difficult days when I dwell on what has happened and at those times the only thing that keeps me going is the thought of reconciliation, no matter how remote it might be. Otherwise it would be almost impossible to bear.

Writing the book taught me that I was a good mum. Hopefully I'd done a good job of raising my children; Jemma, Fern and Rebecca. Although over the years my work took me away from them, they knew I was always there to support them. Recounting the events in my life made me realise that as a family we had been through some very tough times. I learnt that I was a survivor and that you can survive anything if you have the right frame of mind.

Looking at it now I guess you could say I had become a tough old bird! I grew a thick skin but underneath that I was still the same soft squidgy Sally I had always been. I weathered a few storms and came out the other side smiling. As I developed more of a public profile after *Star Psychic* the natural result was that I came under more criticism from people who didn't believe I was genuine, despite all the evidence from the shows. I accept that what I do is not going to please everyone and not everyone is a believer; there will always be cynics. That's fair enough. I didn't have a problem with that at all but sometimes that cynicism boiled over into plain nastiness. That was the nature of the work. Writing the book helped me cope with it because it made me realise that I had survived far worse.

People always asked me whether cynics and sceptics bothered me. My answer was simple: they have to be there. Things always need to be questioned, especially when they defy logic. Sometimes it wasn't nice facing the doubters but on the whole, if it was a controlled debate that didn't get nasty and personal, I was up for it. At the same time I was not a guinea pig. Some people called for me to take part in experiments in a lab. I explained that if they wanted to look at my work and analyse it they should come to the shows and see for themselves. There were all sorts of devices employed by the cynics, even a $1million prize offered to anyone who could prove they were psychic 'under satisfactory observation'. It was a silly gimmick. I figured I might just as well offer £1million to the first person who could prove to me categorically there wasn't an afterlife!

The book came out in September 2008 and was

a hit straight away, so much so that the publisher asked me to write another two. *My Psychic Life* went straight into the Sunday Times Best Seller List, which must have upset a few cynics. Oh well, never mind! I remember thinking at the time that perhaps things were starting to change. Although there have many great books by mediums over the years, they rarely broke through into the mainstream book charts. Usually they were placed at the back of bookshops in dusty Mind, Body, Spirit sections, shoved away somewhere and classified as a niche interest, but *My Psychic Life* was different. Thanks to the fact that I was on television I had a fan base that extended beyond specialist interest.

I did several newspaper and magazine interviews too and at book signings people queued up to see me. I found myself being offered other television opportunities; I was asked to go on game shows and chat shows. It was the first time people had had a proper glimpse of my life and my background.

The attention was generally welcome. People were friendly and genuinely interested in my work. It was refreshing as it hadn't always been that way. Many years previously I'd had my first taste of the kind of extreme character my work can attract.

It was the early nineties and I'd taken on a new client. One of her friends had recommended me to her and from the minute she called, she was pushy. Even back then I was lucky enough to have a waiting list and when she rang to book John took the call.

'The earliest Sally can see you is two weeks on Thursday at 3pm,' he told her.

'But I need to see her sooner,' the lady insisted, 'it's very important.'

'I do appreciate that,' said John patiently, 'but she doesn't have a spare slot in her diary until then.'

'I can pay extra. What about weekends? Can she see me this Sunday?'

'No,' explained John. 'Like I said, she is booked up for the next two weeks.'

Finally the woman accepted what my husband was telling her and booked in to see me. When she arrived, she was flustered and agitated. She waited in the front room of the house while I sorted myself out and when John showed her into the office where I did the readings she started firing questions at me, asking about me and my gift. It felt like an interrogation but I answered openly and honestly enough.

'But this reading is about you,' I said after a while.

As I started reading for her she continued to interrupt and talk. She had wild eyes and a facial twitch; she looked intense and manic. I sensed she was confused and possibly not the full ticket. As I got hit after hit from the spirit world I sensed an older lady in spirit who was particularly concerned about the woman.

'Mum!' she cried, throwing her hands in the air. It made me jump.

When the reading came to an end she carried on

talking and it was all I could do to gently usher her out of the door to make way for the next appointment. After she'd gone I breathed a small sigh of relief; she had been hard work.

I didn't hear anything from her for a couple of weeks but then the calls started. It began with one or two abusive messages left on the answerphone and soon became a daily occurrence. She kept calling and calling. We had about ten phone lines in the house at the time and she would use them all. The messages were rambling. She called me every name under the sun, said I was evil and a witch and that I was going to burn in Hell. She didn't leave a name but the caller's identity was very obvious; her voice was distinctive. When she had booked the initial reading she had left a phone number and an address. We also made sure we had people's details in case the appointment needed to be changed and for safety reasons too – after all, we were bringing strangers into the house. So John called her and told her to stop but she just laughed and so the campaign of hate continued. I became increasingly concerned; I would look over my shoulder when I left the house, frightened she'd be waiting for me somewhere with a knife in her bag. She obviously had issues and so initially I was reluctant to get the police involved but after two weeks we had to get a lawyer involved and sent her a letter explaining that if she persisted with what she was doing, we would report her to the police. Thankfully that did the trick and she stopped calling.

The year continued to go from good to even better when we received some wonderful family news: my daughter Fern and her partner Daren were going to get married. They had been together for many years and had their own family but had never got round to tying the knot. Daren always joked he'd only pop the question after Fern's mum had her own television show. Well, now I had so he had no choice!

Their sons George and Arthur were nine and four, Fern was 29 and she had wanted to get married before she was 30. The timing couldn't have been better. I was lucky enough to have some savings in the bank and I wanted to make sure she had the wedding of her dreams.

Call me old-fashioned but I liked to feel that I could contribute, even though nowadays it's usually the happy couple footing most of the bill when they get hitched. But I was only too pleased to help. I have never been able to save – money has always burnt a hole in my pocket – so when Fern and Daren announced they were engaged I couldn't wait to get involved. I was probably a little too enthusiastic, diving in as if it were my own nuptials.

'Whatever you want, you have,' I told my daughter, getting carried away. I was more excited than she was and I stuck my nose in everything – dresses, catering, venue, invites. Mother-of-the-bridezilla, that was me! I have to say that Fern was very happy to let me have a say and was involved in all of it; Daren left everything up to her.

I think part of my enthusiasm was the opportunity to give my daughter the sort of white wedding I myself had never had. I went with her to buy her wedding dress and there were two she looked fabulous in so I wanted her to buy both of them and decide later. She thought I had completely lost the plot.

As I said earlier, I met John at a New Year's Eve party. We got chatting and I felt an automatic connection with him. He was shy at first but he soon warmed up and we spent the evening joking and talking. We had a lot in common and knew the same people.

I liked John from the first time we met and when he plucked up the courage to ask me out on a date I accepted. Soon we became an item. In those days when you dated, you went steady – there was none of this flitting around young people seem to enjoy today. We didn't have dating apps like Tinder or Plenty Of Fish! Back then it was all much simpler: you met a man, if you liked him you courted and eventually you got engaged. Engagement meant marriage; you got engaged and you set a date. It was statement of intent, not an excuse to buy a ring.

And that's how it was with John and me. After 18 months of dating we were serious and increasingly we discussed the future. At the time we had mutual friends who had just bought a house in Fulham. In those days everyone rented flats – they were cheap to live in, so to have a friend who owned a house was a big deal. Our friends asked us if we wanted the flat they were moving out of;

it would be our first home together. It was a big decision for us both and we talked around it for days. In those days if you moved in with each other, you were pretty much married; it was a big commitment.

One evening we went to see the movie *The Exorcist* at a cinema in Leicester Square. It was a big film at the time and quite controversial because of the subject matter. Everyone was talking about it and obviously given my ability I was interested in seeing it. We settled into our seats and I grabbed John's arm when the horror started. Let's just say that as the story unfolded and the projectile vomiting and possession appeared on the screen it wasn't what you'd call a classic romantic date.

There was an interval in the middle in those days where you could buy an ice cream or have a drink so we went to the bar. Our conversation turned to the flat.

'What do you think, John, should we have it?' I asked, absent-mindedly.

'No,' he answered. 'I think we should get married.'

I did a double take – it was a bolt out of the blue.

'Really?' I said, wide-eyed. Even though we'd discussed a future together I hadn't been expecting him to pop the question in the middle of *The Exorcist*.

'Yes,' he nodded, smiling. 'Don't you think it would be better if we were married and moved in together?'

I knew I wanted to spend the rest of my life with him but I had already been married so I had some doubts. John knew that I had briefly been married before and he understood.

'I don't know,' I hesitated.

'I do,' he said. 'I want to marry you, Sally.'

I looked into his eyes. It sounds corny but I saw my future: John was a kind, fun, caring man. My instincts told me he was the right man for me and soon after I said yes.

It didn't take us long to arrange things. John was quite well off, he owned a greengrocer's shop and he paid for it all but we didn't spend loads of money – weddings were quite low-key affairs in the seventies.

Our wedding day was lovely. I have such fond memories of it. It wasn't over-the-top, it was different then: it was simple. I wanted a long dress, which I bought after John gave me the money for it. It wasn't expensive. The only thing that really mattered was that everyone had a good time.

We had a cake and food at the venue. In the weeks running up to the wedding John bought booze and we stocked the bar with it to save money.

There was one other thing I wanted and so I asked John: 'Can we stay in a hotel on our wedding night?'

We never stayed in hotels so that was the one luxury I wanted us to treat ourselves to on our special day.

'Leave it to me,' said John. 'Is there anywhere in particular you'd like to go?'

'The Savoy,' I immediately said.

Now I don't know why I said The Savoy. I'd never been there but I knew it was a posh hotel in Central London and it sounded like a nice place to stay.

John nodded.

I didn't think about it again until the night of the wedding. Everything had been such a dream. It was a lovely day, one of the best. I still smile when I think about it now.

When it was time to leave the reception the best man offered to give us a lift to the hotel.

'Are we going to The Savoy?' I asked excitedly.

'No,' said John. 'I got somewhere a little bit nearer.'

It made sense and by that time I'd had such a wonderful day I wasn't at all bothered what hotel we stayed in so long as it had a big comfy bed, nice fluffy towels and bathrobes.

The drive there took about ten minutes and we pulled up outside a nondescript concrete building on a grimy main road, somewhere between Fulham and Hammersmith. It wasn't what I had in mind for my wedding night. I won't name the hotel because it's still there, so I'll call it 'The Fleapit' instead. That's all you need to know.

I tried to hide the disappointment on my face when I walked into the lobby in my wedding dress. We were shown to our room, which was cramped and had two single beds in it. You couldn't even push them together because there was a headboard on the wall in the middle with a radio attached to it.

'Did you tell them it was our wedding night?' I asked John as he placed our overnight bag between the beds and sat down on one.

'I did, but the matrimonial suite was taken,' he said.

I was exhausted so I told him I was going to have a shower and then we'd snuggle up together.

As I turned the tap on in the bathroom I heard a familiar piece of music coming from the bedroom. It was the *Match of the Day* theme tune! John had turned on the TV.

When I got out of the shower and went back into the bedroom he was under the covers fast asleep. He looked so peaceful I left him. I climbed into the other bed, turned off the telly and light and went to sleep. That was my wedding night.

The next morning I attempted to squeeze a last bit of luxury from our nuptials.

'Shall we get a taxi back home?' I asked John.

'OK, we'll hail one outside,' he replied.

We went out onto the main road. I had my wedding dress over my arm. As we stood on the pavement with the traffic rushing past John spotted a number 74 bus, which just happened to stop outside our flat.

'Let's get that instead,' he said. He set off after it, waving for it to stop. With my dress flapping in the wind, I ran after him.

So that was the start of my first day of wedded bliss. After that we had two weeks off, which I spent decorating our new home.

Fern's wedding was a bit different. This time there was no expense spared. The venue was Pennyhill Park in Bagshot, Surrey, a beautiful five-star luxury spa hotel. She had two amazing dresses (she couldn't quite decide so I got her both). Her hair was done by my friend Denise McAdam, the royal hairdresser. We had a wonderful sit-down meal with over 100 friends and family. It was an incredible day.

It sparked so many wonderful memories of our own wedding that John and I resolved soon afterwards to renew our vows on our 40th anniversary. Very few people make 40 years and are young enough to celebrate so we wanted to make the most of the opportunity.

People often ask me what the secret of a long and happy marriage is. Honestly, I don't believe there is one. I think you need perseverance. I know that doesn't sound particularly romantic but the reality is that you will face some really tough times and there will be plenty of hurdles. There have been times and circumstances in our marriage that have pushed John and me to the edge; times when if we hadn't had a degree of stubborn resolve we would have split up (more of that later). For us perhaps the secret was that when those difficult times happened, they were not caused because someone else was involved: we have always been faithful to one another. Our difficulties were caused by money, work or the stress of having kids.

I have never wanted another man and I don't think John has ever wanted another woman. He is loyal enough that if he ever felt like straying, he'd tell me first before anything happened. I know he loves me. We have a laugh and we bicker but I've never loved anyone like I love him and it's the same for him. If you are loyal enough to come through those situations they make you stronger. Most of the time relationships can be repaired if both parties are willing and there is enough love. It's when another person enters the equation that you get problems.

Chapter 8
A warning

By 2009 the tour was well established and at the start of the year we had well over 150 dates booked at theatres all over the UK. That number increased to 197 by the end of the year. People loved the show. Even if you weren't interested in the spiritual or the spooky stuff it still offered an entertaining night out. Each night was full of emotion: there was laughter, there were tears and above all there was hope. My show introduced some people to the theatre who had never been before. I had fans attending several shows a year – I called them my 'Psychic Junkies'.

Theatre managers were coming to me and asking me to take my show to their theatres because I earned them money at a time when it was in short supply. The whole country had been plunged into recession and people were cutting back on luxuries and nights out. Everywhere venues were closing down and fewer and fewer people were going to theatres but it seemed that I had hit on something; my show bucked the trend. I started the year feeling very excited and positive about the future.

In February I went back on the road and was booked up until the end of June. Then there was a natural break for the summer when theatres traditionally get quiet – or go 'dark' as they say in the business. After the break I would head back out and was booked up all the way through to December, when panto season started. Some weeks I had six shows booked back to back in different parts of the country. We tried to organise things strategically and book shows in regions further away from home together in a block. Inevitably it meant a lot of time sitting in cars, travelling and staying in hotels and B&Bs.

I finished gigs and I was famished. We'd leave a venue and immediately I would look for the nearest chippie. I learnt all about the regional differences too. In the South they closed early and the choices were limited; in the North they stayed open late and I was spoilt for choice, with curry sauce or gravy for my chips.

I was so excited I didn't notice that my baggy stage outfits were starting to get a little tighter or that I was puffing a bit more than usual when I had to walk up stairs.

Behind the scenes things were happening too. ITV were very happy with what *Star Psychic* had achieved and they wanted to do another show with me but their programming schedules were limited. Budgets were tight and while ITV was a broadcaster with its own channels, it also had production companies within it that made shows for other broadcasters. I was called to a meeting with ITV executives who told me they had been contacted by a TV company who were looking for a show that would recount how a psychic went about his or her work.

'You'd be perfect for it, Sally,' I was told.

That's when the idea of *Psychic Sally: On The Road* was born.

'We'll send a crew out with you to film the shows and there will also be a reality element,' they explained. 'We'll film behind the scenes to show what goes on in your day-to-day life. We'll also get you to do some celebrity readings.'

It was a no-brainer: the idea was simple and brilliant because it fitted in with what I was already doing. As was the case with *Star Psychic*, no money was offered, budgets were tight and I wasn't about to give up my stage shows for a non-paying television show. Being filmed on the road meant I could get on with my life: the TV crew would follow me, not the other way round.

'What will the "reality" bit entail?' I asked innocently.

'Oh, just a bit of scene setting to show you coming out of your house and going home at night,' they explained.

I was excited and more than happy to go ahead but there was one condition.

'I'll need to speak to John. He comes with me so he'll be on camera too,' I explained.

John said yes and that's how simple it was. They wanted eight one-hour shows and they needed to film two theatre shows to give them enough footage for a one-hour programme.

A film crew from ITV came and did some test filming. They filmed John and me in the rose garden at home. At one point I was talking to John as I walked away from him back in the house, asking him a question. As usual he wasn't listening – he was just standing there, looking at the roses, in a little world of his own and ignoring what I was saying. It doesn't sound funny but on screen it looked hilarious. The programme makers loved the interaction between us. It took several months before everything was agreed and while deals were made behind the scenes, I carried on touring.

I loved touring and I soon got to know all the different theatres. Some of them had an energy all of their own, the old ones oozed it; the older the building, the more psychic energy it retained. And when they were filled with people who were all open to spirit the energy fizzed through them. I loved doing the northern dates in big cities such as Birmingham and Liverpool; I also loved appearing in Scotland and Ireland. Some of the theatres held up to 3,000 people.

The theatres responded to the people in them. They slowly started to breathe as they filled up. Empty, they were cold and lifeless. They're not meant to be empty. But as soon as the people started to filter in they roused and swelled with life, warmth and energy. Backstage, I could feel the anticipation grow, along with the noise level.

I started to develop rituals and, along with my own small crew, fell into an easy pattern of work.

'Team Sally' knew its stuff when it came to stage-craft. When we arrived at the venue it was all systems go. We met the theatre manager and my production manager talked through timings and sorted out any props and stage backdrops. John set up the merchandising stand in the foyer and I found my dressing room and got ready. Usually I was deep in the bowels of the theatre, more often than not next to the loos! Most of the rooms were painted plain white, with a mirror and a dressing table, and that was about it.

It became second nature. I'd mainly stay in my dressing room and chat on the phone to friends and family before getting dressed in whichever outfit I chose. I put on my make-up and had an assistant, Julie, who helped out and did my hair. John and the team flitted in and out and then, with about an hour to go before the show started, the team gradually wandered off to do their jobs while I got my quiet time. That was the time I valued most; it allowed me to focus and quietly prepare myself for the evening's show. I sat there in my dressing room listening to this growing buzz, wait-ing for the show to start. That was when the voices and the messages usually started to come through. I could feel them and hear them in my head. As the audience began to arrive, so did the spirits, ready to be hooked up with loved ones once again through me.

And that's how it was in April 2009 in a theatre in the North of England. The day had run like every other day on the road so by rights it should have continued like any other night, there really wasn't anything to mark it out as particularly different. Although we'd had a five-hour drive from our last venue we'd been blessed with light traffic and good weather.

Sitting in my dressing room I checked my hair and brushed down my jacket just as a knock on the door broke the silence.

'Sal, we've got ten minutes before curtain!' my assistant Julie called from behind the closed door.

'OK, love, I'm ready,' I answered.

The door opened and Julie came in, smiling. She's my little pre-show angel is Julie. She makes sure I get to the stage on time and in one piece and gives me the once-over before I go on to make sure I look presentable and there are no stray labels hanging out.

As we walked off I started to feel a pain. Not a terrible agonising pain, but a niggling ache in my hips and knees. But it was nothing to do with pre-stage nerves, it was to do with size. For months I'd been ignoring it, but it hadn't gone away. The unhealthy lifestyle on the road was taking its toll. Now I was tipping the scales at around 20 stone. I wore size 28 clothes and at 5ft, I wasn't just overweight, I was morbidly obese. And that ache was my hip telling me I wasn't getting any thinner.

To this day I'm still adamant that psychologically I never had a problem with being a larger lady, even though I had dieted loads over the years.

John loved me the way I was and I didn't look in the mirror and weep. In fact, I didn't even possess a full-length mirror. The trouble was, even though I was happy being who I was, my body wasn't happy; it was decidedly unhappy. And it was increasingly telling me how unhappy it was.

The touring really wasn't helping. I was spending hours each day cooped up in a car and then on stage on my feet. The walks to the stage each night through the warrens of backstage theatre corridors, up and down narrow staircases, were becoming harder and harder. Most nights I reached the wings puffing and I'd have to stand there and catch my breath before going on stage to meet the audience. Every now and then when I should have been meeting the audience with a wide friendly grin to make them feel at ease, the first thing they saw was a grimace as my hip flared up and reminded me, from under the layers of fat, that it could only take so much punishment. I'd started to lean a little more heavily on Julie for support up the stairs. My breaths were shorter; every now and then I'd give a little grunt.

Following Julie as she shone her torch through the darkness I limped on, trying to put the pain to the back of my mind and focus on spirit. But that particular night was different. As I stood in the darkness catching my breath and aching, listening to the video montage playing on the screen on the stage, one thought, one voice, kept reverberating in my mind.

'You can't go on like this, Sally. You can't go on like this, Sally.'

I remember it so clearly, like it was yesterday. It was a male voice, stern and authoritative, but also full of love and concern. And I knew straight away who it was: my Grandpa George. My mum's dad, he was a lovely man. He died of cancer but when he was alive we'd always shared a special bond. He owned a big working-men's cafe in Hounslow, Middlesex, and I used to work for him every Saturday and throughout the school summer holidays. I worked there through most of my teens. He was a kind man and funny, without realising just how humorous he could be, which made him all the more endearing. Grandpa lived for his horse racing and loved a punt on the gee-gees. He always had the racing papers and studied form like it was a science. And that night he was telling me enough was enough. He was warning me that I'd reached the limit of what my body could cope with and if I didn't do something drastic, and quickly, I'd be joining him in spirit.

Several years earlier I'd suffered the minor heart attack but I'd done nothing about it. Instead I'd chosen to ignore it, putting it to the back of my mind, and carried on as normal. I'd played fast and loose with my health and now it was coming back to haunt me – literally. This was the moment, with the ghost of my grandfather echoing in my mind, that I realised that I was dying: I was eating myself to death. I also realised that larger-than-life Psychic Sally's days were numbered.

I must have gone pale because Julie was looking at me with a frown on her face. She knew there was something wrong.

'You alright, Sal?' she asked.

'I can't go on,' I told her.

She panicked.

'What's wrong? Are you OK? Are you feeling ill? The montage is about to finish, the theatre's full, everyone's paid and they are in their seats. What are we going to tell them?'

'I don't mean I can't go on stage,' I reassured her. 'I mean, I can't go on like this,' I said, pointing at myself. 'I have to do something and I need to do it now.'

And with that I walked out on to the stage, leaving Julie standing there in the wings in the dark, wondering what the Hell I was going on about.

Chapter 9
Speed demon

By April 2009 things had reached the point of no return. The irony was that I was enjoying more success than ever. The workload was gruelling and ultimately it was contributing to my weight gain because of the unhealthy lifestyle I was living. Each year I was putting on a few stone and at my heaviest was 23 stone. I couldn't see just how dangerous and desperate things were, I was too caught up in everything else that was going on. It took my guardian angel granddad to give me the kick up the backside I needed. His message that night was a warning: I needed to get myself sorted out otherwise I'd be joining him in the afterlife. So that night after the show, with John in the car on the way home, I brushed away the tears and told him I had made my mind up: I needed help, I needed surgery. Change or die, it was an easy choice.

'I can't carry on doing this,' I explained. 'I want to be around to enjoy life and to see my grandchildren grow up. If I continue like this for another year it'll be too late and I will have done too much damage to myself. It's not about vanity, it's not because I'm unhappy or I don't like who I am, I need to do this to survive. I'm going to have surgery.'

And John wasn't blind; he could hardly miss the fact that I was getting bigger. Every now and then he'd comment that I was gaining weight but he was happy as long as I was happy. Once I'd told him what I wanted to do, as always he was 100 per cent behind me.

'I want you to be here too, Sally. I'll support you whatever you decide. Ultimately all this means nothing if you are not here with me,' he said, gesturing around the inside of our new Range Rover.

So it was settled. It was my last resort. The following morning I called Alberic Fiennes, the consultant I had been referred to several years previously, and made an appointment to visit him at his clinic. He was an expert in keyhole surgery and, at the time I saw him, had carried out over 1,000 weight-loss procedures and had also trained countless surgeons in gastric techniques.

I went back to see him as a private patient in April 2009. He had a practice at St Anthony's Hospital in Cheam, Surrey, just a few miles from where I lived. I'm a huge supporter of the NHS; always have been, always will be. It's a marvellous service and a credit to the nation. But along with the success that I had been enjoying came a better income that allowed me the luxury to consider going private. And part of me did think that I had got myself into the mess I was in, so I should be using my own money to get myself back out of it. Even though I maintain that morbid obesity is an illness and in most cases there are deeper underlying issues that cause it, I still felt happy to take responsibility for myself and pay for private treatment.

At the clinic Alberic listened intently as I discussed what had been going on since we last met. He was pleased to see that my cardiac problems were under control. Once he had weighed and measured me he confirmed that I had put on an enormous amount of weight. He was quite honest about it. I explained how debilitating my size had become. Just a few days before the appointment I was on stage and had accidentally dropped a photograph I was holding. I was so large that I couldn't even bend down to pick it up. Mortified, I had to call Julie from the wings to step out and get it for me. There was an embarrassing silence in the auditorium while the audience waited for her to come to my rescue. I made a joke about it but inside I wasn't laughing.

My hips and bottom were now so large they formed a ledge around my middle. Eleven and a half stone overweight, I was practically disabled. Whenever I was onstage it was like I was carrying a fully-grown man. The physical effort put a huge strain on my heart and my joints. As we talked Alberic reiterated what he'd told me years before, that there was still just one option for me: a procedure called a proximal gastric bypass. From my medical history he knew that I had tried everything; I'd been on every fad diet imaginable. Then I admitted to him a dark secret from my past.

'I got hooked on pills. It was speed. I was given it to lose weight and I took it regularly,' I explained.

Alberic nodded. He'd heard similar stories from many of his older patients.

When I was in my early thirties I was given a regular supply of amphetamines to suppress my appetite and raise my metabolism. They were the sort of tablets doctors prescribed but supplied for a price at a high-street diet clinic and I became reliant on them. I heard about the place through word of mouth; several of my friends went there. You needed an appointment to visit and were met by staff in medical-looking white tunics.

When I first booked an appointment, I weighed 14 stone. I saw a friendly consultant, who weighed and measured me, and we discussed my eating habits and lifestyle. I'd tried dieting for years. Always I managed to shift a few pounds but then, after a few months, I'd give up and the weight would go back on with a few extra pounds for good measure. It was classic yo-yo dieting.

At the clinic I was given a month's supply of pills called Tenuate Dospan. The consultant explained that they would help suppress my appetite. When it came to drugs I was naive; I always have been. But I had an idea that the pills would do more than stop me from feeling hungry. About a year after I got married and had my daughter Rebecca, I started putting on weight and a girl I was working with at the time offered me something called a black bomber.

'What is it?' I asked.

'People take them when they go out to help

them stay awake but really, they are slimming tablets,' she explained matter-of-factly. 'Just take one, that should last you all weekend.'

'What do you mean?' I asked innocently.

'It will keep you awake for a few days,' she laughed.

That Friday I took it and the girl was right: I didn't sleep for three whole days!

I was expecting something similar with the Tenuate Dospan but assumed since they were being handed out by someone who looked clinical, the side effects of sleeplessness would not be so strong. Having paid £30, I was given my supply in a plain white paper bag.

But I was wrong about their strength. After the first dose I couldn't stop talking, I couldn't sleep and my sex drive went through the roof: I had to do it there and then. John loved it! Over the following weeks I'd take a tablet and we'd be up all night long. I started with one a day but that soon went up to one and a half tablets. Then I lost my appetite as advertised and I did lose weight – whether that was as a result of my appetite being suppressed or all the extra activity, I don't know. It was probably a combination of both things.

Every two weeks I went back to the clinic for check-ups. After the first month I was given another supply of pills. I increased my own dose. Each day I swallowed several of the white pills. The staff at the clinic advised me to eat three meals a day but I was never hungry. I started to crave the pills when the effects wore off. They made me hyper. I talked, I fidgeted and I became anxious when the effects wore off.

Meanwhile the weight continued to fall off me. I would buy a pair of jeans I couldn't fit into at the beginning of the week and I knew by the weekend I would be able to wear them. Now I lived off black coffee, talking and sex. There were days when exhaustion finally took over and I stopped taking the pills and slept for long stretches at a time.

It became a habit that lasted for decades. On and off, I took diet pills for 25 years. Heaven knows what effect they had on my heart and my blood pressure. When the Tenuate Dospan began to have less of an effect I was given another amphetamine-based drug called Ionamin. This was banned in 2000 after fears it could lead to heart disease and because it was being distributed by slimming clinics without the associated risks being explained. It was reinstated in November 2002, but as a prescription-only drug.

When the clinic I initially attended closed the lady who ran it continued practising from her home and dished out pills there. One day I lost her number and I was climbing the walls because I had to have my supply.

I then found a Harley Street doctor, who gave weight-loss injections. They were delivered with a vitamin jab. His practice closed down too. Over the years I visited a network of clinics, doctors and weight-loss experts and tried everything. I lost weight but then I put it back on. The truth is, no one wants to be fat. You might be happy when you're eating cake, you might look in the mirror and say, 'I have lovely eyes and a nice smile', but when you look at the rest of you and it's big you always wish you were smaller.

At times I would come off the pills and think, 'I am going to do this sensibly'. I would cut down on the cakes and the fatty foods but would end up putting on 10 pounds. Each time I stopped it was harder and harder to keep the weight off so I grew.

I craved them when I stopped but I was a mum with kids and sometimes I just couldn't afford them as my children's needs came first. And eventually it just became too hard to get hold of them. I also started to learn more about what they were and the dangers they posed. But when I stopped taking them, I ballooned.

Alberic had heard similar stories many times before. He knew the best option for someone who had reached the stage I was at was drastic surgery so he explained what he was proposing.

'The advantage of a bypass is that it is a direct treatment of the problems that affect the patient and make them overeat. After the surgery food will no longer offer emotional gain, the subsequent weight loss will almost become a side effect,' he said.

What he meant was that I could no longer gorge myself to feel better because physically I would no longer be able to overeat. Food would no longer offer any comfort. In fact if I ate too much, it would offer discomfort.

In detail he explained the procedure. Using a series of tiny instruments fed inside me through a series of small incisions he would section off a tiny portion of my stomach, about the size of a golf ball. The rest of my stomach would still remain inside me, but would no longer function. Food would no longer be able to get into it. The baby-sized stomach pouch would then be re-attached, bypassing a small percentage of the rest of my intestine. My insides would be re-plumbed.

'It's the most effective treatment,' he told me. 'Diet and exercise will not work for you because of the weight you are.'

'How quickly can I have it done?' I wanted to know.

Alberic laughed.

'There are still processes we need to go through,' he explained.

Over the following months I had two appointments with a psychologist, who had to make sure I was mentally prepared for what would happen after the surgery. The op has a profound effect on the lives of those who undergo it. It's not an easy fix. There were a range of very unpleasant side effects and Alberic needed to make sure I was in the right headspace to go ahead. I was, and we fixed a date for January of the following year. Once that was done I began to tell the people I worked with about my plans. Many of them were shocked.

'But, Sally, you are great the way you are. You don't need to change,' they insisted.

When I told them about the impact morbid obesity was having on my health they soon understood, though.

One of my management team at the time expressed concern about the impact the subsequent rapid weight loss would have on my psychic gift and also on my fans. Size had become part of my personality: I was big and bubbly, larger than life. This particular person was concerned that if I suddenly shrank to a normal size, people might think my personality had changed too. Like Samson losing his hair, there was a bizarre concern that if I lost my girth, I might also lose my powers.

But my preoccupations with weight loss and surgery were soon eclipsed by my professional life. The final details of the TV show had been fleshed out and after a summer break in 2009 I started back on tour with a film crew in tow. Living TV had bought the broadcast rights and once the contracts had been signed, the crew arrived at my front door and became a regular fixture of life over the following weeks.

They had a huge handheld camera and arrived with a sound engineer. There was also a producer, a producer director, technicians and runners. Usually there were up to seven people and they were all young and lovely. They worked so hard and put in long hours. After they had filmed a few shows the footage was sent to a studio to be edited and the voiceover was added. The process was like a production line and I had no say in how the footage they shot at the shows was edited. When it came to the reality part of the filming I was happy to play along with it. They made suggestions as to what they wanted to film. Mostly it was innocuous stuff.

'Can we film you in the car?'

'How about you both leaving the house?'

The only time I had to put my foot down and say no was when they asked to film John and me in bed.

'Who'd want to watch that?' I laughed.

They arrived early in the morning and no sooner had I opened the door to them than they had the camera up and running; they knew what they wanted and what would work for the viewers. I had nothing to hide so I allowed them to film whatever they wanted.

After a few days I almost forgot they were there. John and I didn't change the way we behaved in front of the cameras; we carried on as normal. We bickered, we teased one another, we argued and sometimes we shouted and screamed. The crew loved it. You could see their faces light up sometimes. Naively, I didn't realise whether any of it would make good telly.

'Will you leave that in?' I asked after one particular squabble.

'Maybe,' the director shrugged.

John seemed to particularly enjoy the process.

He pretended he didn't, but he soon cottoned on to the fact that he could present himself as the hard-done-by hubby. They definitely developed a little monster in him and he played up to it – he loves a bit of sympathy. He was doing all the lugging and the merchandising.

The presence of a camera crew did not affect the stage shows, though; it had no effect on the energy I channelled onstage or the messages I received. It was good to have the crew there so they could pick up on some of the amazing events that happened and it also allowed me to explain some of what I was feeling and going through as I communicated with spirit.

After a few months I mentioned my impending op to the producer of *On The Road*, Lee.

'What are your fans going to say?' he asked.

I explained that I had to take action because of my heart. Then he came up with an idea.

'You should film it and make a programme about it. Explain to your fans why you are doing it,' he suggested.

It was a great idea and so we decided to look at the logistics of making a separate one-off documentary to be broadcast after the surgery, which had been scheduled for 23 January 2010. After a few meetings, Living TV agreed to show the programme. They were hoping for big things from me. Already excited about the series, now they had a life-changing documentary to go with it.

Chapter 10
Nil by mouth

As the date for the op drew nearer life carried on as normal. I toured constantly and perhaps knowing that I was soon going to have the surgery, I didn't make a huge effort to lose any more weight. I had appointments with Alberic Fiennes and during one he discussed what measures I would need to take before the operation. I would need to be healthy enough to survive the general anaesthetic and would have to go on a severe liver reduction diet in the weeks leading up to the procedure. All bariatric surgery patients have to do this. It's a low-carbohydrate, low-fat diet designed to reduce the size of a patient's liver to enable the surgeon to operate more easily and to decrease the chances of complications. Usually it's a two-week regime just before surgery and I wasn't looking forward to it.

When December 2009 rolled round John and I had six weeks off over Christmas when the panto season got into full swing. We booked a holiday to Australia to see our friends there and knowing that as soon as I got back I would be on the dreaded diet, I planned a last hurrah: a proper Christmas blowout in Australia, a wine-soaked extravaganza before I was given my new child-sized digestive system. In the weeks before our flight I found myself fantasising about the succulent turkey, the crisp roast potatoes, the sweet roasted parsnips, the pigs in blankets... Roasts had always been my favourite meal and Christmas lunch was rightly the king of the roast dinner, the one time of year when you really could eat and eat, and not feel guilty about it afterwards.

I had one more hurdle to clear before I went, a pre-op assessment at the beginning of December. As usual I was weighed and measured. I hadn't been to the clinic for a few months and Alberic's smile turned to a frown when he checked the reading on the high-tech scales.

'Sally,' he said, 'you have gained a stone and a half since we last weighed you.'

I blushed with embarrassment.

Once again life on the road had taken its toll and I was now over 20 stone. Alberic then checked my blood pressure. That too had crept up.

'If you want the operation on the day it is planned for, you have to start the liver-reducing diet today,' he insisted. 'If you have not lost two and half stone by 23 January, I will not be doing that operation.'

I felt like a naughty schoolgirl who had been caught with her hand in the cookie jar – which to some degree I had. As I walked out of the consulting room my dreams of a Christmas blowout disappeared into the distance. I was angry with myself: I'd let John down. Christmas had always been a huge deal and he and I had eaten every Christmas dinner together since we met. It was always a feast, a huge event. I looked at the diet sheet I'd been given at the clinic: two tins of low-fat soup, half a pint of skimmed milk and three zero-fat yoghurts a day until the operation. I wasn't even allowed juice or fruit. Christmas was cancelled.

But I was determined I would go through with it and when I got home I sent the friends we were due to stay with an email explaining what had happened and asking them for help. I told them that under no circumstances should they offer me any treats and warned them that they would have to stock up on soup. They were fantastic, so great in fact that they eventually found a tin of turkey soup for me to have on Christmas Day.

The long flight over was as uncomfortable as ever. I was bigger than John but he was no whippet either and together we took up a lot of space. There was the ever-present risk of deep vein thrombosis to worry about and on most flights I walked away with huge bruises on my hips, where the armrests would squeeze against me. I always needed a seat-belt extension and hated asking. John, bless him, would ask for me, but it was always embarrassing when the stewardess walked towards me with a luminous belt that screamed 'fat person'. My waist and hips were now over 45 inches wide so I had stopped flying normal class and had to book first or business class, which sounds fantastic but it isn't when you have no other option. It's incredibly expensive and it was still a squeeze.

Eating out in Australia was a problem. I could only eat soup and if it was minestrone I asked the waiter to strain off the pasta because I wasn't allowed refined carbs. The best option was tomato soup but after two weeks of that I didn't care if I never ate it again. It also became a challenge to find suitable zero-fat yoghurt. In the UK it was easy, as most shops sell fat-free Müller yoghurt but in Australia there was no obvious equivalent. I spent a miserable day scouring supermarkets for a brand I could eat and eventually, after several hours, discovered one and bought four weeks' supply.

Given my weight and the weakness I was experiencing as a result of under-nourishment, I was not a fun person to be with. Most of the time I was so tired, I just wanted to lie down and sleep.

On Christmas Day I woke to beautiful sunshine streaming through the curtains and the mouth-watering smell of turkey and stuffing wafting up the stairs. I got up and started the day with a refreshing swim in our friends' pool and then sat down for the first watery yoghurt of the day.

'Merry Christmas, Sal,' I thought wryly.

But for me the real killer was smelling the roast potatoes. They've always been one of my all-time favourite foods and it was torture seeing them and smelling them, knowing I couldn't eat even one.

We all sat down for Christmas dinner and while everyone tucked into a feast, I ate my turkey soup. It was still a hugely fun day and I'd asked from the outset that everyone should treat me normally and not make a fuss. They were brilliant and didn't tempt me. Despite missing out on what I'd always planned was going to be the last big blowout of my life, I still have fond memories of the day, even if I did feel like a condemned prisoner denied his final meal. After the pudding (I had a yoghurt!) I briefly excused myself, went up to my room and stuffed four pieces of liquorice into my mouth – just a little Christmas present to me.

By the end of the holiday I had already lost a stone and, despite the sacrifices, was feeling good about myself. Once I could see that the diet was working I started to get excited about the surgery. As I said goodbye to our friends at the airport I knew we wouldn't see them again for at least a year, maybe two, and it struck me that next time we met, I would be a different person.

'Say goodbye to the old Sally,' I laughed. 'Next time you see me I'll be half the person I am now.'

We all laughed, but I don't think they quite grasped the reality. Neither did I. I'd been so big for so long it was beyond the realms of possibility that I would ever be anything else.

Back home the day of the operation was fast approaching and I was gearing up to start touring again. We had a full calendar of dates, the film crew were still with us; work continued to preoccupy me.

A few weeks before the operation I received an unexpected call from someone I knew could answer any questions I might have about going under the knife. Katie Price was having some problems in her home and wanted to see if I would go along and shed some light on what was happening. I jumped at the chance.

Parts of our meeting were to be filmed for her reality show, *What Katie Did Next*, and also for my weight-loss documentary. She had recently met her soon-to-be ex-husband Alex Reid and he had moved into the house she once shared with her former husband, Peter Andre. The huge mansion was a former nursing home for the elderly. Katie met me at the door, somehow managing to look glamorous with her hair scraped up in a bun and wearing a grey tracksuit. She explained that strange things had begun to happen after she had building work carried out at the property. Her sunbed turned itself on and off randomly, as did the huge TV in her home cinema. Immediately, I felt the presence of a woman dressed in white who used to live in the house. She had been one of the residents and I felt that the building work had disturbed her spirit.

Katie was fascinated and explained how she had always harboured an interest in mediumship. Away from the cameras I gave her a personal reading. Later, we were chatting and I told her about the operation I was having and asked whether she thought gastric surgery was a good idea.

'If you've tried exercise, if you've tried diets and if it hasn't helped and if you are unhappy with yourself, then the service is out there,' she said. 'Look into what you are having done, research it, know your doctor, don't go for the cheapest option and as long as you are healthy and your heart can cope, do it.'

Then she added with a shrug: 'And if something bad happens, you'll be asleep and won't wake up anyway, so don't worry about it!'

I had to laugh.

As well as Katie's advice I also had some pointers from one of my daughter Rebecca's friends, who had undergone a gastric bypass. She explained the technicalities and warned me about the adjustment process I faced after the operation. I would relearn what foods I could tolerate and in what quantities. There would inevitably be some foods I ate pre-op that I would not be able to digest post-op. It would take months, and a certain degree of unpleasant vomiting, depending on how the surgery affected me. Different patients developed different eating patterns.

Days before I went into hospital *Psychic Sally: On The Road* was finally broadcast. It snuck up on me. I'd been so busy worrying about the surgery and getting on with the tour that I'd almost forgotten I was being filmed for a television series. The film crew had become part of my normal day-to-day life and were still filming shows for the rest of the series when the first episode was shown on TV. Most of the time I hardly noticed them; they were part of the routine. They'd follow us around and sometimes suggest places for us to go, things to do. Most mornings they'd ask John and me what we had planned for the day. If they thought it would make content they'd tag along. They didn't intrude in the shows. We had signs up explaining to people that the show was being filmed, one of the range of compliance measures I was required to display. Also, we had to announce before the theatre shows and subsequently the TV shows that they were for entertainment purposes.

On The Road went out on a Tuesday night. I was working when the first one was shown so we taped it and watched it when we got home. Throughout the filming we hadn't seen any footage and we had no editorial control so it was a mystery to us how it would be edited. I have to admit I was a little nervous about how we would come across onscreen. It was a gamble; we could have looked like a pair of looneys.

Truth be told I don't enjoy watching myself on telly and there were times when I saw the first episode that I watched through my fingers, especially the reality parts when John and I were bickering. But my reaction didn't matter; the viewers loved it. Over the following days it became apparent just how popular the show would be. I got call after call from people telling me how much they loved the series. The mix of reality and emotional readings had them hooked.

At the time the psychic television market was niche, to say the least. We'd had *Most Haunted*, which did well, but that was very different. *On The Road* cornered the market. People talked about it; there was a buzz. Those who would never have gone to see a psychic watched it. It created a cross-over, bringing mediumship to the masses.

I hoped viewers realised that I wasn't putting on an act. I think they did, and that was why it was so successful: I was just me being me and John and me being us.

The reaction to the reality part of the series really shocked me: people loved us. They loved the humdrum things we did. They laughed as John waited outside the hairdresser, completely and utterly bored; they laughed at John being cantankerous and me nagging him. None of it was contrived, it happened naturally. John took to reality TV like a duck to water and in so doing endeared himself to my fans, who have now become *his* fans. It gave him a purpose. Until then he had always been in the background. He's the most amazing dad – he looked after the kids when I worked and in many ways he was the better parent. I could never have done what I do now when the kids were little without his help: we are a team.

In the days after the show John started to get recognised. With his characteristic tummy he's very distinguished-looking! The first time he was recognised was in Southend. We were in a theatre there and John was setting up the merchandising stall before the show. A group of women came up to him to say hello. Later, some others wanted their photographs taken with him. As time went on, he had all sorts of requests: women wanted to kiss him, one even asked him to sign her cleavage!

Even now, years later, we are still baffled at how people can remember what John says on the show, word for word. Not only do they remember what he says, they also remember how he looks at me, his disdain and his reactions too.

Viewers loved the interplay between us. They would tell me how certain scenes reminded them of their own relationships. During one segment I went to cuddle John and he pushed me away – he's not a tactile person. After that episode was broadcast a women at a show told me: 'That's my husband, it's exactly what he's like.' People could totally relate to our relationship. They loved the fact that John wore tank tops but called them 'sleeveless jumpers'. Also, like their husbands, he spilt food down the front of himself and called the stains his 'dinner medals'. They can see traits of their husbands, dads or granddads in him. Everyone recognises someone like John.

The film crew did a great job of making the everyday highly watchable. They had a daily storyboard we were never aware of and would focus on themes. One day it was sweets. We were in Liverpool and they came up to me and asked if John likes sweets.

'Oh yeah, he loves sweets, he's always in the sweet shop,' I said. 'I never eat them.'

Then they suggested to my son-in-law Daren, who was with us at the time, that he should take John to a sweetshop. He did, and they filmed John coming out. He was surprised to see them and looked guilty. They asked him if he often buys sweets.

'No,' he shook his head. 'I don't eat these sweets, Sally loves them.'

They edited the piece and it was hilarious, like we were both trying to cover up our sweet addiction and blame each other.

On another occasion we were in Scotland and I was going to have my hair done then John and me were going to have some lunch. John was waiting, bored as usual, and the crew suggested there was a cafe around the corner. He is diabetic and was getting peckish so they persuaded him to order a huge egg mayo baguette. They waited until he was eating and asked him how often he had to wait around for me. He spluttered his answer through a mouthful of food.

'I'm not happy,' he said, 'I'm always waiting around.'

I came out of the hairdresser's to find him sitting there, eating.

'What are you doing? We are going to have lunch now,' I scolded. 'Look at you, you have mayo all round your mouth!'

It was exactly the sort of exchange normal couples who have been married a long time have. That's what everyone loved.

I started to get loads of fan mail. People sent lovely pressies, like bangles, necklaces and flowers. At the stage door there were always letters. When the show came out there were ten letters at every gig. Most asked for readings. Every time I went out, I was asked for autographs and selfies. In M&S, in Tesco, in cafes and bars...

The viewing figures were amazing. Normally a show broadcast at that time on that channel would average 70,000 viewers. At its peak *On The Road* got 650,000. This led to another tour and the tickets sold out in days. There was a day when, over a 24-hour period, my theatre shows outsold One Direction and Paul McCartney.

It wasn't a slow process: I jumped in at the deep end. I was normal(ish) the day before the programme came out and the day after my life wasn't normal anymore. It did change family life – I used to be able to pop over and see the kids but all that changed. Life became a bit more complicated; it was harder to do the normal things. Everything took a bit longer because I would have to stop and talk to people. In the days and weeks that followed everything just went whoosh! There were interviews to do, shows to get on with, and then the small matter of life-changing surgery to attend to.

Chapter 11
Under the knife

Before the operation there were two things I wanted to do: I wanted to buy a dress that I would be able to fit into after the operation and I wanted to have a family dinner.

Why a dress? Well, hard as it is to imagine, I hadn't worn one for 30 years. I lived in trousers and tops. At size 26, any dress would have looked like a tent on me. So to motivate myself and to give myself a taste of how the new Sally would be shopping, I went to Peter Jones department store in London and chose an outfit. It was estimated that within three months of the op I would get down to a size 16, which seemed surreal. I spent the afternoon rifling through the racks, looking for something I would be able to fit into.

I found a sparkly, knee-length dress but I couldn't imagine that I would be able to wear it. I felt like I used to when I was a young girl playing dressing up with my mother's oversized clothes, except now the situation was reversed: I was the one wearing the huge clothes.

I got quite soppy when the shop assistant carefully folded my purchase and put it in a carrier bag. For so many years the prospect of wearing something shapely and modern had been laughable, I had stopped even fantasising about it. I'd resigned myself to a lifetime of baggy outfits. I did a quick mental calculation and worked out that in order to get into the dress I had just bought, I would have to lose an inch a week for the next 12 weeks. It seemed fanciful and exciting at the same time. And the amazing shrinking Sally would not stop there.

Alberic had taken measurements and looked at old photographs of me to work out what my final post-operative weight would be. He estimated I would get down to around 10 or 11 stone and be a size 10 to 12. My body would get smaller and smaller until it found its natural size. I might go a few pounds over or under that natural level, but I would always hover around the same weight.

The liver reduction diet worked. I lost two stone but my body was still suffering under the strain of my weight. The last show before the op was in Dartford, Kent, and as I got in the car to drive there, I stumbled and nearly fell. My thighs were so big I couldn't get into the car properly. Perhaps because I knew the next time I would stand on stage I would be a new person, I found that last show particularly emotional. It was a sell-out and the audience were warm and responsive. All the way through I was aware of the ache in my hip and knees and was thankful for the interval when I could rest for a few minutes. The effort of spending two hours on my feet was killing me and as the applause rang out at the end of the night I managed an inward smile. It was as if I had reached the end of a long road. I'd done countless gigs and had been getting larger and larger because of them.

Back at home I arranged the second of my final wishes: a family meal with John, Rebecca, Fern and Daren. The film crew were there and sitting round the table with the cameras and lights, we all felt like we had stumbled into an episode of *Come Dine With Me*. I cooked a huge roast dinner and greeted my beautiful daughters at the door with a kiss and a hug. I didn't want the evening to be sentimental but had asked them round because it would be the last chance for us all to be together before the surgery. I never really had any worries that anything would go wrong during the operation, I had complete faith in Alberic and his team and I had a clean bill of health as far as my heart was concerned. However, nothing is 100 per cent certain in life and it just felt right to be close to my family before I went into hospital.

As my husband and children tucked into chicken and all the trimmings, I sat at the head of the table and sipped my soup. When conversation turned to my weight, Daren was his usual direct self, bless his heart.

'You brought it on yourself really,' he said. 'If you eat too much and don't exercise, that is what happens.' He agreed that the surgery was a life-saving measure. 'You don't see many overweight pensioners, do you?' he explained.

As we talked I noticed Rebecca was becoming increasingly quiet. While Fern has always been the outspoken one, Rebecca is a more sensitive soul and so I turned to her and asked what was wrong.

Her eyes welled with tears.

'I don't want you to have it, Mum,' she said. The sobs started to come in waves. I hugged and soothed her and told her everything would be OK and that the procedure would be giving me a new lease of life.

'Just thinking about you having the operation makes me worried,' she admitted.

Fern concurred.

'Mum, whenever something happens to you, it always happens in extremes. You don't get a cold, you get pneumonia,' she said.

They weren't putting my mind at ease. Fern wasn't wrong; it was the regular bouts of pneumonia that led to me being referred for surgery in the first place. Rebecca explained how sad it made her feel that after all these years and after trying so many times to lose weight I needed to resort to such drastic measures.

'I know you need it done and I know you will be a different person afterwards,' she said. 'But aren't you just a little bit worried that something might go wrong? I know I am.'

I tried to calm their fears.

'I wouldn't be having this done if I didn't need it,' I told them. 'And if I don't have it done then something bad definitely will happen – I'll die, no question about it.'

For once John was the voice of reason. He too

was becoming emotional. The doom-laden fears of my daughters were not helping matters.

'She needs it,' he said, 'no ifs or buts. It is the last resort.'

Later that night, as I lay awake in bed thinking about the evening I realised how much I'd put my family through. They'd missed out on so much because there was so much I couldn't do. I didn't go for walks with them and if we ever went shopping together, I needed regular sit-downs. Reflecting on all those missed opportunities filled me with guilt; the surgery would be as much for them as it was for me.

The day before the operation there was no last supper, just some chicken broth. I had my final check-up and the film crew came along to record it. We were all in good spirits. Alberic's wife and assistant, Louise, was there. She took me aside and reassured me that everything would be fine. The operation was so close now, I asked if it would be better if I stayed in the hospital overnight – I was that keen to get it done. It was scheduled for 8.30am the following morning and I'd have to book in around 6am.

'I might as well just book in and spend the night here,' I thought. But Alberic was adamant that I would be more comfortable at home.

That evening the girls called and we had a brief chat. I tried to make the night as normal as possible. After watching a bit of telly I went to bed, falling into a fitful sleep, where I dreamed of the new, slim me.

At 5.30 the next morning the camera crew arrived to follow me to hospital. Having them there took my mind off what was to come. I hurried around, packing my bag for my stay, and went through the paperwork I needed to take.

As I rifled through my medical folder, by now stuffed full of forms and fact sheets, one form caught my eye. It was a disclaimer warning of the risks of surgery: *The risk of death is of the order of 1%*, it informed.

'That's not too bad,' I thought to myself.

I read on.

> *There is also a significant risk of major complications, such as bleeding, leakage of staple or suture lines, perforation of the stomach or bowel, infection or peritonitis. Together the likelihood of these risks amounts to 10–15%.*

'Not so good,' I thought.

The form was thorough and went on to explain that not all surgeons agreed that the procedure I was having should be done using keyhole surgery. It also outlined the long-term implications, which I already knew but seemed starker when written down in black and white:

> *You will need to remain permanently under the follow-up of a specialist. You will be permanently dependent on vitamin supplements, which may occasionally need to*

be given by injection. Some dietary habits may result in unpleasant symptoms called dumping or in severe cases diarrhoea.

I put the form away and zipped up my case. Taking a deep breath I reassured myself I was doing the right thing and got in the car with John and a cameraman. He and I made idle chit-chat on the five-minute drive to the hospital.

It was still dark when we pulled up in the car park and at such an early hour the place was quiet. The catering staff were preparing breakfast and I could smell bacon and eggs wafting from the canteen. I hadn't been able to eat for 24 hours. Once inside, I met Alberic and his team and had a short chat before getting into my surgical gown. He explained that because the operation was being filmed, the crew would not be allowed in until I was gowned and prepped for surgery. This was to save my dignity for I would be on my back in stir-rups during the procedure.

'They'll only be allowed to film from the waist up,' he reassured me.

Because I would be lying down for several hours and my heart rate would be slowed by the anaes-thetic, there was a risk I might develop deep vein thrombosis (DVT) so I needed to wear stockings – the kind you are recommended to wear on long-haul flights. They struggled to find a pair big enough to fit me and I was too fat to bend down and pull them on. When the nurses eventually helped me into them they were so tight they had to come off again. Eventually I was fitted to a pump machine that enclosed my legs and created pressure.

With the crew following me I was full of bravado and excited about what was going to happen. John was quiet – I could tell he was nervous. He had gone pale, a sure sign he was worried. We had about an hour on our own and I busied myself unpacking my bits and pieces. One of the nurses came in to discuss what was going to happen.

'You will have a line in your neck,' she explained. They needed to feed a tube into the main blood vessel to my heart in case something happened and they had to get medication into my system quickly.

After that, John and I hugged and I rubbed his back. He whispered to me that everything would be OK and that I would see him as soon as I came round. I knew he was scared and it made me feel nervous. I started to get weepy but pulled myself together before the crew arrived.

With a deep breath I set off for the operating theatre. The film crew were in their gowns and waiting in an anteroom when I arrived; the atmosphere suddenly shifted. The normally lively crew were quiet and the doctors and nurses were seriously preparing for the operation ahead. A nurse led me to the operating table. It looked like the type of bed used in maternity delivery rooms, where the bottom half comes away and stirrups attach to the sides. I looked around and saw the theatre lights and the instruments laid out on trays. It started to hit home what was about to happen. Suddenly, away from the cameras and the people I knew, I felt vulnerable.

I lay down and the anaesthetist came over to introduce himself and explain to me what would happen. He was a wonderful, warm man with a calm bedside manner. I could feel myself getting upset.

'We are just going to give you a little injection to relax you,' he explained, lifting my hand. 'It will help you sleep.'

I started to cry and a nurse stroked my hair and reassured me everything would be fine.

As I lay on my back, looking up at the anaesthetist, I could see an elderly, grey-haired woman standing behind him, looking over his shoulder. I hadn't had the injection so I knew it was not a dream. The lady spoke.

'You will be fine, my son will look after you,' she said.

I blurted out: 'I can see your mother.'

The anaesthetist's face changed.

'How do you know it's my mother?' he asked with a frown.

'Because she told me you'd take care of me,' I said.

He smiled. I later learned he had recently lost his mother and she had always taken a great interest in his work.

'We won't let anything happen to you,' he promised as he pushed the plunger on the injection.

By then the cameras were rolling and I turned my heavy head towards them, gave the thumbs-up sign and everything went black.

Chapter 12
The amazing shrinking Sally

I can only remember the hours after the op in snatches. I was kept in intensive care and I slept a lot as a result of the anaesthetic and the painkillers. I remember opening my eyes and having a huge smile on my face. The nurses were surprised because normally, when a patient comes round from a general anaesthetic, they reach for a kidney bowl to be sick in, swear, or say something nonsensical. I was grinning from ear to ear because I had a overwhelming feeling that someone was watching over me. It was my granddad George, finally satisfied that his warning had been heeded.

I was aware of John by my bedside. He asked how I felt and I told him I felt amazing. I had had vivid dreams: I dreamt members of my family, alive and dead, came to see me and congratulate me. The anaesthetist's mother visited as well.

'I told you he'd look after you,' she said.

At one point I was teetering on the verge of diabetes and needed to be given insulin for a few hours to level out my blood sugar levels. I was incredibly thirsty but because such drastic work had been done on my stomach I could only tolerate tiny sips of water. A nurse soaked a small sponge with some mild mouthwash and gently wiped my lips with it to try and refresh me. For a few days all I could manage was small sips of water.

When I tried to move I felt as if I'd done 1,000 sit-ups. I was bloated from the air that had been pumped into my abdomen to inflate it and give the surgeons room to manoeuvre their equipment around inside me. Terrified of splitting my stomach sac open, I nervously sipped small amounts of fluid from a clear plastic thimble.

By the afternoon I was comfortable in my own room with John by my side. He looked much happier, knowing I was getting my mobility and my senses back. He admitted how shocked he was when he first saw me.

After 24 hours I was able to get up and use the loo. Scores of cards, flowers and messages from well-wishers started to arrive.

'No chocolates then?' I asked John. We both laughed.

I was allowed to go home four days after the surgery and soon I was itching to get back to work. I found it very difficult to sit around doing nothing and had to force myself to relax. One afternoon I had a welcome distraction. A journalist from *Woman's Own* came in to interview me about the surgery. The magazine had secured the rights to the exclusive story of my operation and I sat and watched her drink tea and eat biscuits while she asked me all about my journey to morbid obesity and beyond.

In the week after the op I don't remember ever

feeling hungry – it was like someone had pressed the 'off' button in my stomach. The type of procedure I had affects the body's hunger response in ways the doctors don't fully understand. It disrupts some of the nerves running from the brain to the stomach. Sometimes the hunger response comes back, sometimes it doesn't. Even when I smelt cooking, I didn't feel hungry; I didn't get the urge I used to have. I had to keep on telling John I wasn't hungry because he started to feel guilty whenever he ate. Several days after the op I made him a bacon roll, looked at it and thought, 'I don't want that.' I couldn't remember that ever happening before; I'd never turned down the opportunity of a bacon roll.

Remarkably I lost two stone in a week. It was excess fluid. I couldn't stop going to the toilet. It was like I was melting. Bizarrely, this initial weight loss showed most in my feet. They shrank. I remember sitting on the loo, looking down at my feet and thinking how small they looked. Previously a 39.5 shoe, within a week I went down to a 38. My fingers got thinner and I had to have my rings resized.

A week after the operation I was up and about and raring to go. I had shows booked in for the first week of February 2010 but I felt physically fit enough. I had to hugely careful of what I ate and was in constant contact with the clinic.

One day I got a call from Katie Price again – she was still having problems with her spirits. I went over to see her and give her some advice. Her pal and make-up artist Gary Cockerill was there with her. Alex was in the *Celebrity Big Brother* house and she was going through her wardrobe, trying to find an outfit to wear when he came out. She had some amazing clothes, just about every style and colour you can imagine.

'I might be able to borrow some of these one day,' I joked.

She told me that even though it had been just a few weeks since we last met, she had noticed that I was thinner.

A week and a half after going under the knife I had my first night out. John and I went to our friends' house for dinner. I say dinner, but it wasn't a proper meal for me: it was soup. But after nearly two weeks of water and tea, it was a big deal. I was excited and nervous. We chose to stay in rather than go to a restaurant just in case I took a mouthful of something and vomited. Just to be on the safe side our friends provided me with the old faithful – a small bowl of plain chicken soup. Drinking it felt amazing, I could taste every flavour.

John and our hosts had three courses and lasagne for their main meal. I couldn't finish the soup but the evening was a landmark anyway. It felt good to sit down at a table and be sociable over food. It had always been a big part of my social life and I had worried that I would no longer be able to participate.

I started back at work and instead of crisps and sandwiches took jars of baby food with me on the long journeys to and from venues. To begin with I had to eat the jars of food that were completely smooth; any lumps would have come straight back up. I developed a taste for Cow & Gate baby desserts – the label on them said 'suitable from four months'. I'd eat one in the dressing room before a show and have to consume it slowly. It took me 20 minutes to eat one jar and gradually, as the swelling in my stomach went down and the scars from the surgery healed, I was able to eat a bit more and a bit quicker.

When I started on solids again everything had to be cooked until it was soft and mushy. I had to chew each morsel 25 times, taking care not to overload my stomach: if overloaded, it would reject what I'd painstakingly put into it. It was like learning to eat all over again.

A month after the surgery I had a week-long gap in between shows so John and I booked a last-minute deal to Dubai. By that point I could feel that my clothes were slightly lighter and noticed my face was thinner.

The break was lovely. Dubai is an amazing place – slightly surreal and over-the-top. It oozed opulence; everything built there was bigger than anywhere else. A showcase for excess, it was great for a few days' break, thanks to the desert climate but I would have gone slightly gaga if I'd had to spend a long time there.

We stayed in a six-star hotel and the buffet was like a royal banquet, with dish after dish of cuisine from around the world. Strolling through the dining hall, with all the delicious smells and amazingly presented dishes, I did not feel hungry. I looked at the food and fantasised about how tasty it would be, but I did not have the compulsion that I once had to grab a plate and gorge myself. It was a strange feeling.

By that stage I hadn't eaten anything that I would class as proper food but I got brave one evening at dinner and asked John for a mouthful of the chicken he was eating. Big mistake! The piece was no bigger than a thumbnail and I cut it into minute slivers – I must have looked mad. I picked up a tiny piece with my fork and placed it between my front teeth where I chewed it. I didn't want to chew it with my molars in case I swallowed it by mistake before I'd chewed it 25 times, which I had been advised to do. I gulped and had another tiny morsel. After 30 seconds the pain started. Like indigestion, only ten times worse, it built up gradually. At first I didn't mention anything to John and pushed the rest of the food away. I sat there quietly, becoming increasingly uncomfortable. After about 20 minutes the pain was still there and I started to panic.

John noticed something was wrong; I was fidgeting and sweating.

'Are you OK?' he frowned.

'Oh my God,' I groaned, 'something's wrong!' I thought my stomach was about to burst. But John didn't help calm my anxiety. 'I knew you shouldn't have eaten that,' he said. 'Why don't you listen to people?'

I started to work out whether our health insurance would cover the emergency treatment I would need. And as I sat there trying to decide whether I would need to call a doctor, the pain mercifully started to subside. I sat very still, anxiously waiting to see if it would return. John was frowning.

'It's gone,' I said. Then I smiled. 'I'll have an ice cream now.' We both laughed.

Later I learned that the pain was caused by the food passing through the entrance to my stomach. It was painful because my redesigned stomach wasn't yet ready to accept solids. I had several more painful episodes over the following weeks as I slowly started to eat more solid foods and got to grips with my new digestive system. Soon I learnt that eggs were a no-no, pasta and bread too. I vomited often.

I remember having my first roast dinner. It was a quarter of a roast potato mashed in gravy, a tiny slither of chicken and three slices of carrot. For pudding I had two spoonfuls of trifle. We were together as a family, celebrating my aunt's birthday in a restaurant. It was a triumphant moment.

All the pain and unpleasantness was worth it. By March of that year none of my old clothes fitted me. Once a size 26, I was now down to a size 20, which to me felt thin. I had more energy and my body told me I needed to exercise so I started walking more and even went out and bought myself a bike.

Soon I had lost enough weight to get into the size 16 dress I had bought before the surgery. I was still being filmed for the documentary at the time and they decided to mark the occasion with a photoshoot at a studio in Central London. I got the full treatment – a stylist, a hairdresser and a make-up artist. All I could think about was the dress: if I could get into it, it would well and truly mark the beginning of my new, healthier life and the end of my old fat one. Once that dress was on, larger-than-life Sally would be dead. She could no longer put my health at risk and reduce my lifespan.

I got changed on my own, first putting on a pair of leggings and then slipping the dress on over my head. It dropped down over me. Though a little tight, it still fitted me. I couldn't help but cry. The stylist zipped it up and I stared at my reflection in the mirror in utter amazement. The weight was falling off me so fast I barely recognised the woman looking back at me. I hadn't had time to adjust to her. She looked just like me, only thinner; a stranger, but familiar at the same time.

It was a day of emotional firsts; I also wore heels. I hadn't slipped on a pair for 30 years – I might as well have been walking on the moon, that's how strange it felt. Now I was a giddy teenager, growing into a woman all over again. My new clothes revealed shapes I'd forgotten I had.

We had brought along some of my old clothes and held them up for the camera. I couldn't believe that they once belonged to me – they were absolutely huge! I'd lost five stone and part of me was ashamed that I had allowed myself to become so big but the other part was totally exhilarated. I held up one jacket that looked like a tent and remembered when I was so big, I couldn't do it up.

Chapter 13
High energy

The bosses at Living TV were so pleased with the first series of *On The Road* that they commissioned a second before the first one had even finished being broadcast. I ended the spring 2010 leg of the tour with a summer break and headed off to France. A friend of ours owns a villa near Nice, in the south of the country by the sea, and we stayed there for several weeks. Fern and the grandkids came out for a while too.

I had the joy of being able to wear swimwear and not feel too self-conscious about my body. It was a revelation to be able to wear strappy tops and shorts. Previously my suitcases were full of billowy trousers with elasticated waists. It was good to relax in the sunshine for a few weeks because as soon as the summer was over, we were back on tour again until Christmas. The bookings kept coming in and thanks to the boost the television show had given me venues were selling out as soon as the tickets went on sale. And the venues were getting bigger and bigger: the average audience I appeared in front of grew to over 1,000.

The first dates were booked in for September and once again, on the morning of the first show, the ITV camera crew arrived with their equipment ready to plunge back into my strange world. It was the same faces, which was good – we all knew each other and we were all comfortable in each other's company.

Touring had become my life. Initially I set out on the road as a gamble and I thought maybe I could sustain one or two years as a theatre act. I'd assumed I'd play smaller and smaller venues as interest dried up and would eventually go back to doing private readings from home. But after two years the opposite had happened. Demand was higher than ever and no sooner had I appeared at a venue than the management there were asking me to rebook. Now I appeared at some venues twice in a year; unheard of for even the most popular shows let alone stage psychics. I started to realise that for the foreseeable future my career was probably going to be as a touring act.

Theatres liked us because we were simple to deal with. My show didn't have a big stage set – just me, a backdrop, a bowl for letters from the audience and pictures and the camera crew, We travelled light and set up our own merchandising stall. I didn't have a long rider full of diva demands. All we requested was parking spaces for two cars and a van; I even took my own kettle. I had a little box for touring – it had tea bags, water and, before the op, some biscuits.

The recession that had the nation in its grip didn't seem to affect ticket sales. People were looking for hope and positivity in their lives and I think that's why psychics are not usually affected in times of uncertainty: they offer something spiritual. I noticed the same in the 1980s when there was a recession: people want faith and optimism, they want to know everything will be OK. Psychics are reassuring. We let people know there is something else and that we are all surrounded by love and support.

By the time we started back in theatres the film crew had got the measure of what they needed to make the show. They chose which venues to attend. Usually it was the bigger ones and it was there that the most energy was generated: energy equalled messages. My rapid weight loss had also provided me with renewed energy and this definitely helped hone my gift. Now, more than ever, I felt more aware and awake and open to spirit. Even before I arrived there I would tune into the psychic energy of a venue. I would start to pick up messages and sense spirit on the journey to work. When I was onstage the messages were increasingly vivid; I would see and hear things with incredible clarity. Often they made me jump because they were so clear it felt as if they were happening on earth plane – the realm of reality where we exist. At one show the spirit of a black dog shot across the stage, flew into the audience and landed on its owner's lap. It looked so real, I screamed. I could have reached out and stroked it. It was right there in front of me but I was the only person who could see it and I was flabbergasted.

It has always been my belief that if you trust in spirit and open yourself to it, it will come to you and show you signs. I must have been an open book because things happened, on and off stage. The energy buzzing through me started to affect things offstage too.

On one occasion we arrived at a big old country house hotel in the Midlands after a gig in Birmingham. It was capacity crowd of around 2,000 people. I was exhilarated but exhausted at the same time because it had been such an amazing night. The hotel was a Georgian stately home, full of history. I love old hotels and we used this one regularly when we were in the region. We arrived around midnight. The driveway to the front was lit atmospherically with yellow lamps. I felt a little tingle at the back of my neck as we drove up the pathway but I wasn't spooked. Usually I get feelings about old buildings because the psychic energy that surrounds everything seeps into them – they are like sponges. John and I were taken to our room on the second floor somewhere by a lovely German porter; it was a bit of a warren.

As soon as I walked into the room I noticed the prints on the wall. They were of old-fashioned garments, dresses and suits. I commented on them.

John and I went to bed. In the middle of the night I woke up and heard a popping noise. I felt there was someone in the room. Half asleep, I shook John to wake him up.

'Can you hear that?' I whispered.

He grunted. The noise continued. It sounded like it was coming from the door and moving across the room towards the bed.

I shook him again.

'There's something in here,' I insisted.

He woke properly.

'Don't be silly, go back to sleep,' he told me.

Eventually the noise stopped and I drifted back to sleep. When I woke at about 6am I was a bit disorientated because I was in a strange room so I got up and rolled the blind up slightly to let in some light, then went to the bathroom. I left the door open and as I was sitting there, half asleep, looking out into the bedroom, my eyes adjusted to the gloom. On looking at the prints again, I couldn't focus properly as I wasn't wearing my glasses.

I went back to bed and slept in until 9am, when I got up and took a shower. When I had finished, I put on my glasses and glanced briefly at the wall. I did a double take: the pictures were different, they all looked odd. Then, when I looked closely, I realised they had been turned upside down. I took the one I was looking at off the wall and as I did so, I noticed that the wire across the back that hooked over the nail in the wall and held it up was still bent in the same shape as if it had been hanging normally. It didn't make sense; it was bizarre. I could hardly speak.

'Look at this, John,' I said.

He was staring at the pictures too. 'Someone's playing a trick on us,' he frowned. 'That's impossible.'

At breakfast I told the receptionist.

'What room are you in?' she asked.

'203,' I answered.

She looked puzzled.

'But 213 is our haunted one,' she explained.

Fascinated, she went back up to the room with us to investigate. When we tried to get in the lock wouldn't work. She went back down to get another key but before she came back up the door inexplicably opened. When she came back, she looked around the room and at the prints in particular. She was as puzzled as we were. We examined each frame closely: there was a thin film of dust around each one, which would have had fingerprints or marks on them, had someone taken the pictures off the wall. There were no signs of any disturbance. And as we were looking at the pictures the popping noise started again. I nearly jumped out of my skin. After a few seconds it stopped again. Completely baffled, we left the room.

There was definitely a ghost in that room. I think it wanted me to know it knew I was there. We'd stayed at the hotel several times before and had never experienced anything spooky. I think maybe the ghost came up to our room to say hello: it saw me in the room looking at the prints and realised they were a way of getting my attention.

It happened in dressing rooms in old theatres too. I had a ritual: I put my towels down and put my make-up on them, always in the same way. There was always a work surface and a mirror and I always put my towels and make-up on the right-hand side of the mirror, probably because I'm right-handed. Once I had set up, usually I went to do a soundcheck on the stage and signed a few books for the merchandising stall. On several occasions I would return to the dressing room and my make-up had been moved to the left-hand side of the mirror. It was a sign; it was their way of saying hello, we are here.

The more I worked in large venues, the more adept I became at handling the messages that came through. I would work two or three messages at a time. One message would snowball into another and several would share a common link; I was transfixed by the process unfolding around me. To begin with, when I started touring, the links had appeared irregularly and haphazardly but increasingly they became more pronounced. I later coined the term 'message building' to describe what was happening. The psychic energy built up as my accuracy grew; spirits were drawn in.

It always started with a clear hit, a very specific message taken by a receiver. A hit is a piece of information I am given by spirit that is so targeted and appears so random to anyone else that it can only be meant for the receiver: it is what spirits use to validate themselves to the people they are linking to. A hit is the type of in-depth message that people are blown away by. I believe hits make connections between the spirit and the receiver so strong that they anchor the spirit to the world of the living and send out a signal into the afterlife that there is a powerful link that others can use. In life it is human nature to want to communicate with one another and to share ourselves as we are sociable creatures and the same is true in death. Think of it like a bar or a restaurant – the ones that attract the most custom are the ones that have customers already in them. Most of us would walk past an empty restaurant because it would have no atmosphere. When we see somewhere lively, we are drawn in.

Spirits want to connect with their loved ones and if there is an opportunity to do so they will take it. When I was on stage they realised there were pathways and they were drawn to them. They listened in to the messages I was giving and if there was a link or a hook they recognised, such as a subject with which they were familiar in life, they came through too. Each message was a fishing line that stretched out from me and contained pieces of information, which were baited hooks. Others in spirit were drawn to these hooks if they associated with them and when they did so, they took the bait. I started to realise that the whole system was orchestrated because, unbelievably, there were increasing clusters of people who had things in common but didn't know each other sitting near to each other in the audience. As the links between the spirits and their loved ones increased, so more were attracted to the area in which the links were being made. There were some spectacular readings and the film crew delighted in picking up on the reactions of amazed members of the audience.

When series two of *On The Road* was broadcast in 2010 it built on the success of series one. The formula remained the same but if anything, the series contained slightly more reality. Programme makers knew how popular the reality part of the show had become and realised that viewers related to the interplay between John and me so in series two the reality part was as important as the shows themselves. Everything shown was genuine; there were no retakes and certainly no trickery. The footage used from the shows was all authentic and at the very start of the process I explained to the production company that they would only get one chance to film messages: all the reactions were true, there was no playing it up for the cameras. You can't play it up and I certainly couldn't stop mid-flow to go over things again or to let the cameraman get a better angle!

As the series progressed I noticed something strange was happening... well, stranger than the discussions with dead people! When I was out and about, I wasn't recognised. After series one I couldn't buy a pint of milk without someone asking me for an autograph or a selfie. But as series two progressed, it was John who got all the attention. After a few days I realised why: it wasn't that he was more popular than me, even though he was developing his own little fan club. It was because he is more recognisable. You see there was a gap of several months between a show being filmed and being broadcast and in those gaps I continued to lose weight. And I was losing it fast. The Sally on the telly looked very different to the one in the mirror who looked back at me every day and people just didn't recognise me. It was funny: people would approach John, say hello to him and blank me.

We were in Belfast one day. It was drizzling and I was wearing a coat with the hood pulled up to cover my hair. As we walked past a shop, a man emerged and recognised John.

'My wife is going to your wife's show tonight,' he explained.

John smiled.

'Your Sally is an amazing woman,' he continued. 'It's grand that she's come over to Northern Ireland to do a show. Will you wish her well for me?'

'You can tell her yourself, she's right here,' said John, pointing at me.

The man blinked.

'Surely that's not you,' he said, peering under my hood.

I pulled it down and smiled.

'It's not Sally,' he insisted, 'there's nothing of you!'

'It *is* me,' I laughed.

'What happened to you?' the man frowned. 'Are you OK?'

'Never better,' I smiled.

It happened repeatedly. A few days later I was back in the UK and shopping in Kingston when a bloke came up to John.

'Mr Morgan, I love the show,' he said.

'Thanks,' I said, but it didn't register with him who I was.

Later that month I had a gig in Southport and whenever I played the town we stayed in a hotel called The Vincent. They knew us by sight because we'd stayed there several times but when I walked in, the girl behind the counter didn't recognise me.

I started to enjoy my newfound anonymity. Now I was free to wander round the shops, unimpeded. I could whip round Marks & Spencer in double-quick time. At each show there were always a few seconds of confused silence after I walked out on stage while audiences tried to work out where Psychic Sally had gone. Then the rumours started to circulate that I had contracted some kind of terrible illness. The truth was I had never felt better so I introduced a new section into the introduction of each show in which I explained about the surgery and the drastic change in my appearance. As far as I was concerned I had nothing to hide. I had undergone a procedure for the sake of my health that was life changing and I wanted to celebrate it, not deny it. Anyone who has had gastric surgery has every right not to speak about it but I felt that as it had such a visible effect people were bound to ask and if I denied having had it done then it would send out the wrong message to other morbidly obese people.

I had nothing to be ashamed of – and neither did anyone else who considered having the operation for the sake of their health.

Chapter 14
Woman versus food

The new fitter me came at a cost. As well as the unpleasant symptoms of stomach pains and vomiting that some foods sparked, I also suffered hair loss. Before the op I was warned about it but that didn't make things any easier when my locks started coming out in handfuls.

I had regular post-op check-ups and during one a nurse explained what was happening. Apparently a lot of people suffer some hair loss after major surgery due to the stress of the procedure. Mine was compounded because I developed protein malnutrition, a common side effect of gastric bypass procedures. As my body was digesting less protein than before, it was trying to preserve the small amounts I did eat. And it was closing down bodily functions that used protein but were not essential, including hair growth. My hair went into a resting state, so instead of growing normally, it fell out. I was assured I wouldn't go bald but words cannot describe how horrid it was to run my hand through my hair and feel it come out in clumps and to wash it and see the plughole clogged with it. Thankfully, after a few weeks things eventually stabilised and I stopped moulting.

The year after the op was full of little weight-loss

victories. Certain events stood out; small steps for most normal people, but huge leaps for me. One Saturday night I decided to have a bath. Nothing amazing about that, you're thinking, but I can honestly say it was the most remarkable bath of my life. And it was remarkable for two reasons. I was sitting back in the bubbles, relaxing and reading a magazine, and I'd been in the water for so long it started to get cold. Normally that would have been time for me to get out because it was too much of an effort to turn on the taps. Sitting up had always been a huge effort as I was too big to bend in the middle. If I wanted to stay I'd have to haul myself up by the handles on the side of the bath, then kneel, which was uncomfortable because of the weight I was putting on my already delicate knees, and finally, I would lean forward far enough to turn on the hot water. It was too much effort. Sometimes, when I was feeling really lazy, I would call down and beg John to do it for me. Subsequently, bath times were rarely relaxing or long-lived. Mainly I'd get in and get out before the water got too cold. But that Saturday the water got cold, I put my magazine down, sat up, leaned forward and turned on the hot water. I didn't register what had happened. It was only when I got out and was drying myself off that I realised the significance. My belly – the obstruction that had stopped me from bending forward for so many decades – had shrunk to the point where I had regained some of my flexibility. I called out to John.

'I can sit up in the bath and turn on the taps, I can't believe it!'

'Well done!' he called back.

And then the second memorable thing happened. In the bathroom we had a couple of bathrobes hanging up – I never wore them because I was too big to tie them up at the front. But that night I took one off the hook, put it on and tied it up. Wrapped around and tied, it was no problem. It was the best bath of my life. Then one day I managed to cross my legs. I know how odd that sounds but I hadn't crossed my legs for many years. My thighs were so big there was no way I could lift one over the other. But I was sitting there at home on the sofa and suddenly squealed. I made John jump.

'What's wrong?' he asked.

'My legs, look at my legs! They're crossed.'

On another occasion I was on the sofa and leaned over and scratched an insect bite on my ankle. Another first. Then I managed to paint my own toenails, yet another.

The magazine article came out in which I spoke about my weight-loss surgery and the documentary was broadcast later in 2010. They called it *My Big Fat Operation*, which wouldn't have been my first choice of title but the reaction was great. I started to get wolf whistled when I went on stage and when I met fans at signings after the shows they were fascinated.

Everything was transformed. My face grew thinner, my neck got narrower and the fat on my back started to reduce. Now my wardrobe was full of oversized clothes that no longer fitted me. Many of them were handmade or designer. There was no point in keeping them but I didn't want to throw them out. I thought about taking them to a charity shop but realised they would have been too big for most people and would sit on the racks forever. Instead my daughter Fern sold them on eBay and raised money for charity. She spent hours going through my wardrobe and we selected a few of our favourites to start with. Each month she sold a few and each month we chose a charity.

My touring habits changed too. Before the op I took food with me. I had breakfast at home and then breakfasted on the road. I'd stop at a service station to use the loo and end up buying food. I was constantly grazing and filling up on sweets and cakes and junk. And then suddenly, I no longer had the urge. I had to be so careful about what I ate that I prepared only a small amount of food at home to take with me. My takeaway of choice became a banana. The only luxury I had was sweets and I could only manage one or two of them before the dreaded sugar dumps would creep up on me so I approached them with extreme caution. It was hard because after the op I developed regular cravings for sweets. I'd never been that bothered before but now I found myself carrying packets around.

Sugar dumps were what happened when my blood sugar levels became unbalanced. I was in bed when I experienced the first attack. It must have been about a year after the op and I woke up with my heart racing. Shaking and sweating, I had an urge to eat. I'd been warned about them so I realised what was happening but that still didn't stop me from being terrified. Often I'd have them when I came off stage and my energy levels dropped. I had to sit down and felt light-headed, dizzy and nauseous; I broke out in cold sweats and had palpitations. At their worst sugar dumps felt like having a heart attack. It was a really weird feeling; people would be talking to me and they would sound far away, I had trouble focussing.

Once people knew about the op they would talk to me during line-ups and signings. Often women who had undergone the same procedure themselves would come up and talk to me about it and sugar dumps were a regular topic of conversation.

A fan approached me after a show in Newcastle and explained that she'd had the operation several years previously. She had lost 15 stone. Taking hold of my hand, she pulled me in conspiratorially.

'Are the sugar dumps bad?' she whispered.

'Yeah,' I nodded.

'I think I'm dying when I have them,' she admitted.

We could empathise with each other.

They came on without warning. Sometimes I would wake up at night in the middle of a dump and think I was dying too. I soon learnt that the way to get through them was to eat carbohydrates but in the midst of them I felt so bad it was hard to think about eating anything. Different things worked for different people and I was amazed that I craved the things that would help. My body knew that when I was having a sugar dump, bread would help and I would eat tiny morsels of dry bread and try and get them down quickly so my body could digest them and stabilise. Often I'd eat sweets and then feel the dreaded early signs of a dump. In those situations I didn't tell John because then he'd know I'd eaten too many sweets.

'Are you having one of your funny turns?' he'd ask.

I'd shake my head guiltily but give the game away when I started to speak because sugar dumps had the effect of making me slur my words.

For a long time after the op meals out were a lottery. I never knew how my stomach would react to what I put in it. John would sit there and watch, waiting for beads of sweat to pop out on my top lip. I could never eat much anyway. I'd order a starter, take a few mouthfuls and then push the rest around my plate. Even a small amount of food would leave me with the uncomfortably full feeling I used to get after a Christmas lunch. Eventually my hunger response came back but with nowhere near the voracity of before. I'd burn so many calories onstage that by the time I came off, I needed to eat quickly. Because I ate such small portions, I was hungry every few hours and needed to top up little and often.

As per the instructions of the surgeon I started taking supplements, which I will have to take for the rest of my life. I took vitamin D, vitamin B12 and a multivitamin.

One of the nicest consequences of the surgery was the support I received from fans. Most of them were genuinely pleased for me. Family and friends were very supportive too, some fans not so much.

One woman queued up at a book signing and put a copy of my first book, *My Psychic Life*, in front of me. She pointed at the photograph on the cover.

'We like her,' she said. 'Where's she gone?'

I have a standard response to that kind of reaction now.

'That person had a heart attack. This one here, she doesn't need medication any more.'

Funnily enough it was usually the skinny ones who feigned mock concern.

'Don't go losing too much weight,' they would say.

A lot of my fans are heavy men and women and I feel great empathy for them. Obesity is a disability. A lot of people will mask how they really feel and tell their friends and family they are happy in their skin but it doesn't matter how comfortable you are with your size, eventually it starts to have an impact on health. For that reason, given the opportunity most fat people would lose weight, no one would chose to be ill. Today there is more choice than ever for plus-size people and it is more acceptable to be obese. But it doesn't matter how nice you look, if your weight is affecting your health, it's a problem. I know – I couldn't walk properly, couldn't breathe properly. My body was being crushed; my joints were under so much strain that I ached all the time. Why would you choose to do that to yourself?

I got lots of letters in the years after the op telling me I was an inspiration, that I had spurred others on to do something about their weight. People have told me they have had surgery after seeing what it did for me. Sometimes I wished John would consider it too. I never had a problem with him being a larger man – I love him for who he is, not what he is. However, his health has concerned me. He has Type 2 Diabetes and all the indications that he will suffer from ill health as he gets older, with the classic 'coronary waiting to happen' shape: large stomach, thin legs, thin arms and no bum. But he is terrified of doctors, hospitals and needles. It will take a heart attack to make him lose weight. This has not caused friction between us, though. When I was big, John never told me to lose weight and I'd never tell him. I want him to be healthy but I'll not change him.

People often ask me whether the surgery was worth it. It's an easy question to answer. Yes, it was undoubtedly the best money I have ever spent in my life. I realise how lucky I was to be able to afford it and I think it's amazing that it is available on the NHS.

It took two years until I felt I was living normally with the effects of the surgery. The greatest consideration I had after that was whether or not to have cosmetic surgery. The weight loss left a mark – my skin was like a balloon that was inflating for 30 years, getting bigger and bigger and straining to contain what was inside it. If you let all the air out quickly, the balloon loses its elasticity; the same applies to skin. I have an apron of loose and saggy skin where my belly used to be and so I toyed with the idea of having a tummy tuck to get rid of it. When I put on clothes, the loose skin made it problematic. If I put on a pair of jeans, the skin hung over the top. Reconstructive procedures could fix the problems but as with all major surgery, they were not without risk.

Rapid weight loss after surgery affected my body in many ways and I soon realised why, for most people, surgery was the last resort and a matter of health, not vanity.

Chapter 15
Fans and fanatics

Things just got better and better; I had so much more energy and somehow that made my ability even more effective. I always knew that the spirit world was driven by some kind of fundamental force, a psychic energy that permeates everything and links the world of the living with the world of the dead. This energy flows through everything – through me, through you and through all living things. It soaks into the very fabric of life. The more alive I felt, the more effectively this energy flowed through me. I could control and channel it; I could tune in and listen to the messages transmitted on it.

Everyone has psychic ability. We are all born with it – there is no great secret, it is intuition. It is the ability to listen in to the world around us and hear the messages and see the signs. Unfortunately, over time most of us lose this ability. Modern life drowns out the messages. But with practice we can all develop our psychic side. First, we have to trust in the signs we see and open ourselves up to possibilities. The more we trust in spirit and acknowledge those little inklings and feelings we have that we are not alone, the clearer the links to the other side become. Spirits are attracted to those who are open. If you ignore the signs they send you, then you are, in effect, pushing them away and telling them you are not interested.

Spirits love the energy that life generates and as I became more alive, I believe I attracted more psychic energy. I was fitter and healthier. Sometimes I felt like one of those rods on top of skyscrapers that draw lightning and channel it. I was a link between Heaven and Earth and some amazing things happened during my shows. Those linked messages I spoke about earlier became even more pronounced.

At a show in Perth, Scotland, the image of a broken plank of wood slotted into my mind as I was giving a woman a message. 'Where did that come from?' I thought to myself and so I asked the woman.

'Was there a piece of timber or something that got smashed in half?'

She shook her head, bemused.

There was no doubt about what I was being shown; the image was strong and clear, so I persisted. A spirit then came into focus: a teenage boy. And I knew that he had taken his own life; he had hung himself. He appeared directly in front of me in human form and pulled me to the other side of the stage. I knew he wasn't there for the woman I was giving a reading to so I asked the audience about him.

'I have a young boy here,' I explained. 'I know that he committed suicide. I see a plank of wood and it is broken in the middle.'

The name Daniel popped into my mind and I relayed it to the audience.

'I think he hung himself,' I said.

Then another name: 'Graham?' I wondered aloud.

A middle-aged lady in a purple top stood nervously several rows from the front of the stage.

'Graham was a close friend,' she told me.

I didn't know it at the time but Graham had died in 2004. He lived in a village called Auchtermuchty, close to Cupar in Fife, and within the space of a few years several young people had died in the same area. They had all taken their own lives.

'So who is Daniel?' I continued.

A younger woman, who was with Graham's friend, stood up with her to explain: 'It was the name of his house,' she said. 'It was called Dan's.'

Suddenly I saw the relevance of the broken wood – there is nothing random about spirit. I saw a bench in a graveyard: a memorial bench and the plank across the middle of the seat had been broken.

'If you go to his bench, someone has jumped on it, it's broken,' I told the women.

But the second woman shook her head. 'That's not Graham's bench, that is another of my friend's, they are in the same cemetery,' she explained. 'There were a few of them. They all killed themselves. One of the others had his bench vandalised the other day.'

I was given a date, the 17th. It was the date that the boy with the vandalised bench had died,

17 March. So I had two teenagers in the same cemetery who had lived in the same village and had both taken their own lives. And in the audience I had two women who knew them. You can't tell me there is anything coincidental about that.

And it got even stranger. A while later, at the same show, I picked up the names Gordon, Kerrie and Kirana in quick succession. Immediately a lady stood up.

'My daughter is Kirana, I'm Corrie and my brother was called Gordon,' she said.

Gordon was only 29 and had taken his own life a few years before. He had a message.

'He says he is not cold,' I told the women. 'He says it is just his body that is cold and he is no longer in his body.'

This exchange was captured by the film crew and after the show they caught up with the woman. Through them I later learnt the relevance of this information. Gordon's mum went to visit her son in the mortuary after he died. He looked so peaceful and she bent down to gently kiss his cheek. As she did so, she drew back in horror: his lifeless skin was so cold. She was always troubled by that but had never spoken to anyone about it. It was a moment in her life that I had captured.

Then came another amazing psychic moment. Another name popped into my head.

'Is there anyone called Anne Marie?' I asked Gordon's sister. She turned and pointed to the two women I had been speaking to earlier, whose friends had both committed suicide in Auchtermuchty. Anne Marie was the older woman's daughter. Also in spirit, she too had come from that fated village.

It was an amazing reading, one of the most mind-bending I can remember. All those spirits from that small village had swarmed in that night to let the world know they were safe and sound in Heaven and it was all because I could feel the psychic energy and reading the messages contained in it so clearly.

It was one of the most positive periods of my life. I felt that I was genuinely helping people. The shows were allowing me to reach a wider audience than I ever could at home and each day I was receiving emails and letters telling me how I had given comfort and hope. I was getting compliments too! Someone went up to John and told him they'd seen me four times over the years.

'Each time she looks younger,' the woman said. 'What's her secret?'

'She's married to me,' he replied.

Joking aside, I was happy and that showed. I didn't have the weight on my mind, on my shoulders or on my body.

Throughout that period not everything went perfectly, though. I had some business issues that I had to deal with, and which were not pleasant. But I don't want to dwell on that – it's boring commercial stuff. Suffice to say, in show business most acts come across difficulties in their business dealings.

It's not all roses and for me it was not always an easy ride. At different times over the past few years there were people and arrangements that I was involved in on a professional basis that ran their course. Disentangling myself was frustrating and complicated but ultimately the best thing for me at the time.

The more popular the theatre shows became, the more I attracted attention from what I affectionately call the 'lunatic fringe'. I had people turning up outside theatres I was performing in from extreme Christian groups. Don't get me wrong, I am a Christian and I believe in God. I like to think what I do complements the message that there is life after death but a lot of religious people aren't that tolerant towards those who share the same general view as them but don't subscribe to their belief system to the letter. And so they criticise. It's the same mentality that led to witch-hunts. In one theatre a Born Again Christian group left a pink leather-bound bible for me. Nice gift! Except whoever left it had gone to the trouble of highlighting any passages referring to witchcraft with hearts drawn in red pen. My favourite was Exodus 22:18: 'Thou shalt not suffer a witch to live'. The message was clear and it was quite frightening. I thought it was a really pretty gift until I opened it.

In 2011, series three of *On The Road* was broadcast. At the same time series one and two were repeated and other countries began to show the series too. I also wrote and published a third book,

Life After Death. All that attention, along with a rolling tour that continued to attract devoted audiences, meant that I had my fair share of eccentric fans. And because I wanted to make myself as accessible as possible and meet people after shows at book signings and line-ups, they had an easy way of meeting me.

One woman approached me at a signing after a show with a photograph. She put it down in front of me and pointed.

'It's my living room,' she explained.

I really didn't know what to say.

'That's nice, dear,' I said.

Then I looked more closely at the photograph.

'Oh!' I exclaimed. I shifted uncomfortably.

The woman's lounge was an exact replica of mine. At first I thought it was my lounge until I realised it was smaller. She had copied every single detail and explained to me that she had seen pictures of my front room in a magazine article. I remembered the article: it was about my favourite things and in it there was a photo of me on the sofa in my lounge. Different objects and ornaments were highlighted and I gave a brief description of each one – where I'd bought them and the sentimental reasons why I liked them. This woman, who looked very sweet and normal, liked the décor so much she wanted to imitate it in her own home. She had sourced the same table and got her husband to go out and buy the same shade of paint for the walls. She explained that she had

had trouble finding copies of the two paintings of poppies I had on my walls (I had bought them in a shop in Margate, Kent). But she went on to tell me that she had found someone who was going to paint them for her.

'That's very flattering,' I told her. And it was. She was very nice but in the back of my mind I did think it was extreme and it brought it home to me that maybe I needed to be a bit more careful about what I put out in the public domain in future.

Many times I'd encountered intense people over the years. To a large degree it came with the territory. When you profess to speak to the dead you must expect a certain degree of criticism and to have to deal with extreme people. Being a psychic is a lure to certain people, like putting cheese on a mousetrap. I'd already had the client who crossed the line and became fanatical and eventually threatening and abusive. Frankly she was nuts and that was the first time I said to John, 'Whoa! We need to be careful about who we let in the house.'

Then there were the sceptics and cynics. They were always there and the more my public profile grew, the more they directed their attention towards me. Again, it came with the territory. People would say I was cheating and that what I claimed to do was all a con act. For as long as I've been a medium people have doubted my ability. But that's life – there are people who believe and those who don't. Sometimes it wasn't nice and it did get boring, having to continually defend myself, but on the whole, if it was a controlled debate that didn't get nasty and personal I was up for explaining myself. At the same time I was not a guinea pig to be tested. I told those who criticised me that if they wanted to look at my work and analyse it, go to the shows. By now I had become the country's most high-profile psychic. I'd reinvented the genre and without planning too had dragged mediumship kicking and screaming into the 21st century. There were consequences for being so high profile.

Around this time I was given the chance to do other reality shows too. Three times I was asked to sign up to *I'm A Celebrity… Get Me Out Of Here!* Before the op this would have been a physical impossibility. For a start there's no way I could have jumped out of a helicopter! I was so heavily booked on the tour that I didn't have time to consider it. It would have meant disappointing 10,000 people. Anyhow, I'm not sure I could have done it as I'm terrified of rats and I dread to think how my post-surgery stomach would cope with a kangaroo anus! I was also asked to appear on *Celebrity Big Brother* but I like my privacy too much. I could never sleep in a room full of other people and have to use the same bathroom. The only show I would love to do would be *Strictly Come Dancing* but I'm not sure the BBC would have me because of what I do for a living. It would probably be too controversial for them.

Chapter 16
Moving on

By the spring of 2011 another huge change in my life was taking shape. For a few years John and I had been toying with the idea of moving house. For many years we had lived in the same house in a tree-lined road in a quiet part of southwest London called New Malden. The house was big enough for me to have an office where I could see my clients. We had loved it there. It was the perfect suburban existence but for several years, after I gave up my home practice and went on tour, I had felt that perhaps it was time to look for somewhere else.

New Malden was lovely but I wanted to move out into the countryside. My daughters had long since grown up and had families of their own so there was nothing particularly tying me to the area. Now my work was all over the UK so I didn't have an office I needed to be near. I didn't have to be near a train station either because I didn't commute. Instinct told me it was time to move and I always follow my instinct.

John agreed that it was as good a time as any. The problem we had was that for most of the week we were in different parts of the country and so we didn't have the time to start looking for a property. So we found our very own Phil and Kirstie and used the services of a couple of property searchers who had been busy trying to find something that met our requirements since the end of 2010. We wanted to find the right place because it would probably be the last house we ever bought so I was quite specific. I told them I wanted an old vicarage simply because I love Edwardian and Victorian period properties. With an older property you are going to get big rooms with high ceilings. We wanted to stay near enough to our family but further out of London to benefit from a rural location so we started looking in the areas of Reigate and Redhill. Over the following months, when we had time, we went to see a number of different houses.

We weren't in any rush. After all, we had been in our previous house for 18 years. When we bought it our requirements were very different. At that stage in my life I had a growing client list and saw people from Monday through to Saturday. I would see six or seven people a day and so we wanted somewhere with a separate room downstairs where I could do readings and we also wanted somewhere near a station. That house had lovely memories and remains in the family because our daughter Fern moved in when we eventually moved out. Some houses are like sponges and soak up psychic energy. Our family home in New Malden was just such a property. It had a lovely warm feeling about it and there was also a resident spirit, a ghost. He was the husband of the old lady we bought it from and he'd died many years before we moved in. His wife was in her nineties and in a home when we purchased the house so the sale was arranged through her son and daughter-in-law, who explained that the couple had bought the house in 1932. A lovely family, they were very religious.

The ghost was extremely gentle. Our New Malden resident was very discreet and well behaved. Very occasionally I would catch sight of him in the corner of my eye. He only appeared in the spring and would make himself known through the smell of pipe tobacco. His presence became more pronounced after we did some work on the building a few years after we moved in. When we bought it, the house was clean and presentable but it needed updating. It had a 1930s galley kitchen with pull-down cupboards and a big old porcelain butler sink. We did the work as and when we could afford it and then, when we'd saved up enough, we had the old kitchen replaced and an extension added. He often appeared in the new part of the building, probably to take a look at what had been done. Spirits are naturally curious. He never caused any trouble so I can only assume he approved of our workmanship.

Thanks to my gift I've seen spirits in every house I've ever lived in. Some have been more active than others. After John and I first married we moved to a house that was haunted by a midwife. She was quite mischievous; she liked to make herself known and would often open the windows and turn the television on and off. She liked to wind John up too. When I was pregnant with Fern and suffering from severe pre-eclampsia she tried to look after me. I used to get terrible dizzy spells that made me feel ill and the only thing I could do was go and lie down completely still until the sickness passed. One day, during a particularly nasty bout, I was drifting in and out of sleep when I heard someone walk round the bed and tuck the blanket in around me. Later, when I was better, I thanked John. He looked at me, puzzled.

'I've been in the garden all afternoon. I haven't been in the bedroom!'

On another occasion I was in bed with the television on. Suddenly it switched itself off. It was an old-fashioned TV with a manual switch so it couldn't have been an electrical fault; it was the ghost telling me I needed to rest.

One night she really made a fuss. I have no idea why. We woke up to the sound of banging downstairs. I thought we were being burgled.

'There's someone in the house,' I said to John urgently.

He got up purposefully and made plenty of noise.

'Who's there?' he called.

He walked downstairs, exaggerating his footsteps in an effort to frighten whoever was making the noise. Tentatively, I followed behind. The noise was coming from the backroom and John burst in with a flourish. The window was open and rattling but there was no wind. Puzzled, he walked over to it. It stopped. He turned around to look at me to make sure I had seen it and as he did so, it started up again. We both jumped.

'What the...!' he breathed.

'Whoever you are, please stop,' I said, trying to sound kindly but firm. The window went still. I walked over to it and closed it.

Back then I didn't have the understanding I have now and so the next day I went to the local church and spoke to the vicar about the events at our house. He came round and blessed the house. He made John and me kneel in each doorway and then blessed the room and sprinkled us with holy water. It was a bit of a hoo-ha. Nowadays I'd just ask it to leave nicely.

Altogether our trusty property searchers looked at 147 houses. We looked at one and I fell in love with it and we were preparing to make an offer. But we saw it in the dark and the next day when we viewed it in the light we realised that it was opposite an industrial estate. We were both disappointed as it ticked all the boxes. It was Sunday and we were with our searchers, who explained that one other house was just about to come on the market. They drove us to see it but we couldn't do a viewing as the people who lived in it were not there. It was in a quiet country lane, near an aerodrome, and was a vicarage, right next door to a gorgeous old village church. I knew straight away it was where we would live.

When I was young I had vivid flying dreams. I would swoop through the air and look down on certain scenes. In one dream that I always remembered from around the age of ten I flew over a house on the corner of a country road. There were fields around it, an in-out driveway and a church opposite. In my dream I flew into the belfry of the church and sat there looking at the house. I knew it was the house I was going to live in – it was the house I was looking at on that Sunday afternoon, quite literally the house of my dreams.

John loved it. He loved the garden and even from the outside I got a lovely feeling from it. It felt safe and secure, like nothing could hurt me when I was in it. So the following day we had a viewing and made an offer the next.

We picked up the keys in July 2011 and when the previous owners moved out, I was still on tour, so we waited two weeks until I finished to move in properly. During the time when the house was empty John went round one day to check and have a nose around. Someone had smashed a window at the side of the house and tried to break in. Thankfully a friend of Daren's ran a security firm and so we paid for a couple of guards to stay in the house overnight until we moved in. They slept in the lounge downstairs in sleeping bags. One evening the people who had tried to break in pulled up in the driveway in a white van. They must have got the shock of their lives when two burly men ran out the front door and chased them away.

When we moved in we made two new additions to the family: our dogs, Albert and Martha. We'd had dogs in the past, our last being Harriet the Jack Russell. When she died, aged 18, I said to John, 'We will wait and if we ever move somewhere with a decent-size garden we will get a bulldog.' Why a bulldog? Well, they don't need an awful lot of walking and they have bags of character. A fantastic breed, they are very docile and they love children too.

So when I knew we were moving into the house, which had some land out the back for dogs, I went to see a breeder in Derby when I was doing a gig there. I had been in contact with her online and checked out that she was reputable. She told me her bitch had a litter due and it just so happened that when I was in the area the dogs would be ready. I mentioned this to John and he just said OK – he didn't really think I was serious.

In the weeks running up to the gig the breeder sent me photos of the adorable puppies. I wanted a dog and I picked Albert, but when we arrived Martha was there, watching me talk to Albert. She came running over, yapping. Now I love brindle dogs so I couldn't resist. I bought them both and took them back home to a surprised John, who then had to look after them for two weeks in our old house before we moved. They say dogs look like their owners – well, there was no mistaking who Albert and Martha's dad was!

Eventually we moved into the house. Everything was lovely but there was a lot of work to do. We had the usual teething problems anyone has with older properties. My advice to anyone buying a home would be to go round and turn all the taps on when you view it because the first night we stayed, we got in the shower, turned on the taps and realised the water was just a dribble. It needed to be re-plumbed and because the suite was pink and not to my taste I figured we might just as well have a new bathroom at the same time. And it started from there. We had the kitchen done because it was really old and small. Luckily we saved money on labouring costs because at the time the dogs were cutting their teeth and chewed through all the old wooden kitchen units. Within a month they had destroyed everything. We had upstairs converted into a flat too.

Inevitably the work disturbed some of the spirits residing in the house. Early one morning I woke and I could hear people talking. John woke up too.

'What is it?' he whispered.

It was men's voices. Once again I thought we were being broken into. I got up and went out onto the landing and realised where the voices were coming from. In the spare bedroom someone had put the telly on: they were letting us know they were there.

When we moved into our new house, Fern, Daren and their two sons George and Arthur moved into our old house. They too were getting acquainted with their tenants in spirit.

Fern used to smell the pipe-smoking ghost in her bedroom and her son Arthur often heard someone calling his name. At around 10pm one night Fern was sitting on the sofa in the downstairs back room, where the building work had been done, watching TV. She saw a light flickering on the wall. It looked like something sparkly was reflecting light. She thought it was her watch, but it wasn't. Then she wondered if it was light reflecting off her sparkly mobile phone case. It wasn't. Maybe it was Arthur on the stairs behind her, shining something onto the wall as a joke. But he was in bed. The light faded and then a couple of seconds later there were orbs floating everywhere. They floated for a while and then coalesced into the shape of a man; they all joined together – they were fading and flickering in and out of focus. Then the apparition went. Fern was gobsmacked.

A few weeks later she was on her own in the house, taking a shower. She got out and her dogs started barking (they always barked when someone came to the door). When she went downstairs to see what had disturbed them the tap in the back garden was on full and all the drawers in the kitchen were open.

Despite these spooky goings-on we soon settled into our new homes and our new lives. The dogs became a massive part of my life. I posted regular photos of them on my website and they developed a following on Facebook. After we'd had them for a year we started pining for another one. If I could,

I'd have five of them. So I rang the breeder and she explained that Marley, Albert and Martha's mum were being covered again by a different dog – and that's where Nellie came from. I couldn't resist!

They all have their different personalities and it's hilarious watching them together. Albert was a scaredy-cat, not an alpha male at all. Martha ruled the roost and was very stubborn. Whenever I called her in, she would sit there looking at me. I learnt to walk away and only then would she come in. Nellie was very mischievous. She chewed the walls and her best friend is the cat, Marmalade, with whom she tried to play but she doesn't realise her own weight or strength. I soon learnt that bulldogs never go round things – they walk into them and try to push them out of the way.

Very quickly they got spoilt. They all have little Barbour coats and are walked twice a day. Nellie was very greedy, she'd push the other dogs out of the way at dinner time and eat everything in the bowls. Martha loves Maynards wine gums and boiled eggs but she will only eat the egg if it's runny, sliced up and put in a dish. She will howl for a wine gum but only eat it if it's been partially chewed in my mouth (I know how odd that sounds!). We got them checked out regularly and unsurprisingly they were overweight and needed to have weight-control food. Given my history, I should have been more aware. Despite their size they moved quickly but Martha was born with an elbow displacement for which she had an operation. Before that, whenever she ran, she ran to the side because one leg wasn't right. They were my babies and I adored them.

Now, everything in the new house was perfect. I'd become a proper country lady!

Chapter 17
No business like show business

Throughout 2011 I toured extensively. I did around 130 shows and passed on thousands of messages. Instinctively, I felt that once the message had gone, I had to let it go. Messages were fleeting moments in time, they were not there to be analysed and it certainly wasn't my place to try and re-establish communication with the spirits who had given the messages. They were moments between those in spirit and their loved ones; I was privileged to be the medium through which those messages were given but they were not for me.

I became good at closing myself off to the emotional aspects of the messages. If I took them all on board, I knew it would drive me mad. Perhaps it was a self-preservation thing. I always empathised but in some cases I couldn't help but be affected by what I had felt and heard. As I got older, I found it increasingly harder and more emotional when I was involved with certain messages, especially when I picked up young kids in spirit. Even though I knew those children were safe and in paradise surrounded by love, as a mother and a grandmother I would still be brought to tears on a regular basis.

The unplanned elements of the shows made for

entertaining viewing. Even people who didn't get a message would enjoy a rollercoaster night out. Most nights I surprised myself and would often gasp or whoop when something happened that I didn't expect, much to the audience's delight. I remember one woman who queued up to meet me after a show, who said: 'I'd come and see you even if you weren't a medium. You are so funny, you should have been a comedian!'

I loved having the opportunity to meet fans and do book signings after the shows. It was lovely to chat and have a personal connection with people. I did so many that at one stage I developed carpal tunnel syndrome (CTS), a condition that affects the nerves in the wrist and causes a tingling sensation, numbness and sometimes pain in the hand and fingers. On doctor's orders I was instructed to stop signing books.

I had nothing but admiration for all those who stood up and took messages at the shows. It cannot be easy. No one ever knew what the content of the messages would be and some of the information given to me from spirit was embarrassing, to say the least. Over the years I had learned to grow a thick skin. I have heard it all – affairs, odd sexual preferences, embarrassing body problems. It's hard enough to discuss things like that in the privacy of a consulting office but on tour the details were coming out in front of a live audience. Inevitably, at some shows messages came through and no one in the audience took them. Often spirit would guide me to where the receiver was, but it was never my place to single people out. I would never force anyone to participate. Sometimes I'd point out a general area, though.

'It's for someone over here,' I would say, gesturing to a section of the auditorium. Often I'd see someone squirming uncomfortably or being held back by the person they were with and the spirit in my head would be saying, 'It's her, it's her!' And at most shows afterwards someone would walk up to me and tell me that a message that went unclaimed had been for them.

I could understand the reluctance: it is fear or embarrassment. Some people don't feel comfortable standing up in front of a crowd. It took me some time to get used to it too. The smaller the venue, the more reluctance there was. If it's a small town there is more chance of people knowing each other. When I played Jersey in the Channel Islands for the first time there were several missed messages. I commented on the fact afterwards to the theatre manager.

'It's a very small island and everyone knows each other,' he explained.

Despite the risk of embarrassment, I knew I had to be true to the messages I was shown and describe every thought, voice, word and vision literally as I saw them.

Mostly I was welcomed back again and again. Some venues, however, had a closed-door policy when it came to psychics: they refused to host shows because they believed that the subject matter was too controversial or that it was religious. It was mainly council-run theatres that shunned psychic shows. Some theatres are owned privately and can make autonomous decisions about the programmes they stage; sometimes the theatre manager can exert influence. In other cases large corporations own theatres and the decisions about what shows are hosted where are made in boardrooms, largely for commercial consideration.

My tour followed a pattern. After each break in the summer and over Christmas I started off in smaller venues. They were 400-500-seater warm-up venues, where the crew and me would be able to get back in the stride of things. Each year we did a Scottish leg and played several dates in the country back-to-back. Edinburgh was the biggest venue and the energy there was always electric. The older the buildings, the better the energy.

We didn't have much of a say in the ticket prices as theatres set their own highest rate and they also take a cut of each ticket (one group of theatres takes anywhere between £7 and £12 from a ticket). Very quickly I learnt to have people around me whom I could trust. It dawned on me that I was better off keeping everything in-house. Many artists have lots of different companies doing different things for them but over the years I built up my own office and employed 18 people, which was unusual, but this was learnt through bitter experience. As far as I'm concerned the only way to control things it is to do them yourself.

There are a lot of costs – VAT, the cost of the crew, accommodation, travel, theatre charges, staff wages, tax, my office. They are all slices from the cake and I was left with a sliver. Touring is so expensive that we even considered doing fewer shows to cut costs.

I soon discovered that the theatre could be quite elitist at times. Most of the people I met were lovely and welcoming but even after several years continually touring there were still places where I knew I wasn't accepted. Traditionalists believe the theatre has to be in your blood. I'm not a lovey and even if I'm still touring when I'm 80, there will be people who will sniff at me because I'm not a proper thespian: I'm not in the clique, I'm an outsider.

You get some real characters in the theatre world. A different breed, many of them spend their days in dark rooms out of the sunlight. Some have personal hygiene issues. You see, the theatre is all about show and creating an illusion. The theatres themselves are perfect metaphors of the industry. When the lights are on and the curtain is up they are wonderful places, full of life. Behind the scenes they can be dark, lifeless places, though. Some of them are filthy. Now don't get me wrong, I don't expect flowers in the dressing room, all I usually ask is a clean dressing room and a spotless lav. On rare occasions even that has been too much to ask. I was in one dressing room where the bin overflowed with used sanitary towels. It was gross! The manager tried to argue that the cleaner had been in. And we refused to rebook at another venue because it was infested with mice. At a theatre in Wales I looked out of a window and saw rats running around outside by the stage door. But it's no one's fault – most theatres are housed in old buildings and thanks to cuts in arts funding, many of them are not well maintained.

During my time touring I've got into all kinds of scrapes. On one occasion someone working in the box office of the venue I was appearing at was caught on social media, writing, 'We've got that awful Sally Morgan on tonight. I wouldn't waste my money'. We had to inform the management and she was suspended. After that all the staff were warned not to make comments about the acts. Then we've had managers who try and chuck the fans out before I've had a chance to meet them after the show. On one occasion John was trying to tell a manager that under the terms of the contract we had with the theatre we were allowed to stay and meet fans up to a certain time and that he was being unreasonable in asking us to get rid of them. When John told him how unreasonable he was being, he turned to him and said: 'Do you want to step outside?'

Sometimes they don't help themselves. We played one show in the autumn. The theatre had been dark for the summer months. It was a lovely day, the sun was still out, the theatre had sold 1,100 tickets and there were still 400 seats left. We arrived in the afternoon, looked around and saw there were no posters advertising the evening's entertainment (we'd sent the venue loads of them in advance because we send out all the promotional material). John tried to explain that perhaps it would be a good idea to display some posters and a week later we got a call saying there had been a complaint that we were being rude. Other theatres advertise all their shows for the next three months in advance.

Often John gets the brunt of all this. In one theatre he was stopped and asked for his ticket. He wears a laminate that is printed with the words, *Sally Morgan: On The Road. Access All Areas.*

'I don't need a ticket,' he explained.

'Who are you?' the staff member asked.

'I'm Sally's husband.'

'Anyone could say that,' the woman persisted. During the exchange several members of the audience walked past John, recognised him and said hello. He had to get a few of them to vouch for him.

In 2011, after the third series of *On The Road* was filmed, there were plans for a fourth and people in the production team began to think about other ideas for television series I could be involved in. One possibility was my own chat show. It was an exciting prospect but hard to see how I would fit it in – I was out five to six nights a week and doing around 120 to 130 shows a year.

In September of that year the tenth anniversary of 9/11 came around. I had a lot of friends in

America and regularly went to work there. In the years after the tragedy I saw several ladies who had lost their husbands or partners in the Twin Towers. I used to have a lot of clients who lived in the USA; I gave readings to several Manhattan-based bankers and traders and their wives. After 9/11 there was a general fear of flying and no one wanted to come over to the UK for a few years so I went over there instead, basing myself with a wealthy friend in a place called Westport, Connecticut. I rented a room in a high-end Pilates studio and well-being clinic frequented by several famous people and saw my clients there. Tragically, several of them were 9/11 widows.

One lady brought me a watch that her husband was wearing on the day of his death and which still had his blood streaked across it. When I held it, a horrific image flashed through my mind. I held the lady's hand tightly; she knew what I'd seen and neither of us needed to discuss the details. Her husband had been one of the poor wretched people trapped in their offices. As the fire closed in on him, he had desperately tried to escape through the window. As he tumbled towards his death he struck a sharp edge. The sheer force of the impact tore his body in two. Rescuers only recovered one part of his remains.

'I was lucky,' his grieving widow told me, 'I had something to bury.'

In the USA word spread. I was reading for some influential and powerful people. Celebrities began to call but being America, they had some ridiculous demands.

One day I received a call.

'I represent a public figure, she would like to make an appointment to see you,' the lady on the other end of the line said in an officious tone.

'I'm sorry, love, I'm all booked up,' I told her.

'My client really insists on seeing you,' the lady continued.

I looked through my diary and sighed.

'Perhaps I can fit her in late one afternoon next week. I can move a few appointments and see her on Wednesday.'

For a minute there was silence, then I heard the woman muffle the phone and speak to someone else in the background. She came back on the line.

'That is acceptable, Mrs Morgan, however we ask that you sign an NDA before the meeting.'

'Bloody cheek,' I thought. An NDA or Non-Disclosure Agreement is a secrecy document people are asked to sign, usually when others don't trust they will keep details of meetings confidential.

'I'll sign your NDA after you sign mine,' I countered.

That completely threw the woman. In the end they couldn't agree and the meeting never happened. Her client was an A-list Hollywood actress.

Another meeting that did go ahead was with Courtney Love, widow of the rock star Kurt Cobain. Of course I'll keep details of our meeting secret, suffice to say she was an interesting character!

In the summer of 2011 we had a break in France for a few weeks after a frantic six months on the road and while there, we took stock of things. John was travelling as much as I was and was also taking on more of the business side. It was a strain driving all the time and he needed some more help on the road so we had a family conference around the swimming pool in the villa we were staying in one day. It was a beautiful summer's day and the rest of the family were there with us.

I had a vision to build excellence within the psychic world and I wanted to grow the business from the bottom up. I'd always had a wonderful relationship with my son-in-law Daren and so I made him an offer.

'I need someone I can trust, who can put in the hours and who shares my goals and vision,' I explained. I offered him a job and he became our driver and helped John.

A fully qualified plumber at the time, he was doing well for himself. He needed time to consider the offer. The holiday finished and a week after returning home, Daren called to say he wanted to come on board.

He was a brilliant addition to Team Sally.

Chapter 18
Storm clouds on the horizon

I've never had an issue with growing old. I happily embraced the years and in a professional sense I was getting better with age – I believe mediums have a better understanding of their work when they get older. To do this job you need a gift, of course, and you also need to be able to empathise with people and communicate with them appropriately. Those skills come with age and experience. I'd been through my own ups and downs, studying hard at the University of Life. I had experienced family tragedy through the estrangement of my daughter. My marriage with John had its fair share of ups and downs too. At one point, a few years after the tour began, strains started to appear in our relationship, specifically over a business matter (I must be vague for legal reasons). It was a personnel issue that John and I had opposing views about. Neither of us was willing to budge and although it was a business matter, the feelings it caused spilled over into our private lives. I thought John was being unreasonable when he wanted me to take a course of action regarding a member of the team that I was not prepared to take. He thought I was being naive and difficult. We argued and neither of us was prepared to see the other's point of view. In the end it became so bad I started to question whether I wanted to be with John: he was being unsupportive and coercive, I felt. But events happened that proved he was right and I then conceded I should have listened to him.

Up until that point it was probably the most serious problem we had faced in our marriage. We had been through so much together it would have been foolish to throw it all away. I realised that soon afterwards but in the heat of the moment it's often difficult to take a step back and put feelings aside.

John has always supported me and stuck by my side. Whenever I was criticised he was always there to defend me, and the more famous I got, the more criticism I came in for. There was a group of people – sceptics – who were becoming increasingly vocal in their criticisms of me. Most active online, they had sceptical websites where they posted their thoughts and opinions on web forums. The same people appeared again and again, calling for me to be tested and tried to offer explanations as to how I was doing what I was doing. They didn't accept my explanation that I was psychic.

In all honesty I have no issue with sceptics at all. Everyone has the right to his own opinion. I've often been challenged by them to undergo scientific testing to prove myself. In my opinion I don't need to do this because the proof is there each night I host a show. There is still so much to discover and it would surprise the sceptics to know that I put my faith in science to provide the answers. There are a few brave academics already testing what the scientific community describes as the paranormal; usually their work gets drowned out by the sceptic community, single-minded in their denial of the supernatural.

It's my belief that the key to understanding what the afterlife and the energy that lies at the heart of it all really is lies in the realm of science, possibly an area such as quantum mechanics. There are all kinds of mysteries and mind-boggling puzzles that great minds are trying to unravel at the edges of human understanding. Beneath the border between France and Switzerland, near Geneva, there is the Large Hadron Collider, which is investigating the tiniest fragments of matter to see what lies inside them. Scientists there are hunting for something called the God Particle. Who knows what else they may discover, what other mysteries there are to be unveiled. Science, conducted with an open, inquisitive mind, has the power to answer so much. I sometimes feel sorry for sceptics because they spend all their time denying and don't embrace possibility. Anything seemingly miraculous, groundbreaking and pioneering always gets shouted down by those with a blinkered view of the possibilities of life. It wasn't so long ago in historical terms that people who said the Earth orbits the Sun were called heretics. But just because you have doubts about something, doesn't mean it does not exist. Doubt doesn't mean you should discount something altogether just because you don't understand it. That's where the sceptics get it wrong: they dismiss it as out of hand. We can't see sub-atomic particles and atoms but we know they are there. At the end of the day, when it comes to psychic events and messages from the dead, something is happening and I'm proof of that. But because addressing that means going against vocal sections of society that flatly refuse to acknowledge the afterlife, the sceptics have their own agenda and will refuse to look at the issue objectively.

The ironic thing is that sceptics always do eventually overcome their cynicism when they pass over to spirit. I have had hundreds of them who come through to me from the afterlife. On one memorable occasion a man's three daughters were in the audience. He was a total non-believer throughout his life-time but he came through with his message loud and clear and there was a huge amount of energy radiating from him as he connected with his children. They told me all through his life, whenever he heard about mediums he would scoff and discount them as a load of rubbish. Nevertheless, when it came to the opportunity, he was the first to come through and make contact, even though there were other relatives of the girls in spirit waiting to come through. He barged his way to the front of the queue! I smile when I think what a very pleasant surprise it would have been for him when he passed and realised death was just the beginning.

As I approached my 60th birthday I became aware of something that had happened after one of the shows I did in Ireland. It had been reported in an Irish newspaper that following the show a couple of women who claimed they had attended my show in Dublin had called a local radio station to accuse me of cheating. This was nothing new: I was regularly accused of being a cheat, usually by the aforementioned sceptics. The women only gave first names and left no forwarding details. They told a phone-in show that they believed sound technicians working in a room at the back of the theatre were relaying information to me on stage through a hidden earpiece. They made up a theory that I had people working secretly in the theatre who went round before the show pumping the audience for information that was then relayed to me and used in the show. The idea was preposterous. According to them I would have had to employ a network of spies in hundreds and hundreds of theatres and they would have gone undetected for years. And they would have had to be brilliant at espionage and manipulation because I was getting some very specific hits and some incredibly personal information at every single show. According to the theory then, I was employing an army of superspies able to sidle up to strangers in theatre foyers and persuade them to unwittingly divulge highly personal information. To top it all off, the theory taken to conclusion would mean that when this cleverly collected information was used in a show, the person who had given it to the spies and then stood to take it when I offered it as a message from the dead didn't realise what had happened because in all the shows I'd done, no one had ever come out afterwards and explained that they had recounted the details I knew to a stranger in the bar before the show. Incredible! Even if you were a sceptic, if you analysed the theory given by the unnamed ladies in Ireland with an unbiased mind you might surmise that it was more unlikely than the possibility that I was communing with the dead! It just seemed ludicrous. Anyone would surely realise that one day I would run the risk of blackmail, or of it leaking out. There was also the small fact of a film crew. For several years I'd been followed by a reality crew and surely they would have picked something up?

In terms of being outlandish it was right up there with the suggestion that before every show I tour the local cemetery, looking for freshly-dug graves. And for that reason, although it always hurts to be called a cheat, I didn't think too much about the allegations and got on with much nicer things, mainly organising my 60th birthday bash.

I have always loved throwing parties. I'm not extravagant or a show-off, but I like to host a good bash and I love to watch my family and friends enjoying themselves. The party would give me an opportunity to say thank you to everyone for the love and support they had given me through the years. The film crew and people from ITV were invited, along with my old friends, Darryn Lyons and Mitch Winehouse. I'd also have the opportunity to wear the new dress I'd bought from a boutique in London for the occasion.

Initially, I didn't want a 60th but instead to celebrate as a family we were going on a holiday to Australia together at the end of the year. However, we had always planned a housewarming party and eventually decided to roll the two landmarks together. When we sat down and started to work out who to invite it became apparent that over the years I'd made a lot of friends and the guest list just grew and grew. It soon became apparent that we wouldn't be able to fit everyone in the house so instead we booked a marquee. We also booked a catering truck that would supply fish and chips, jellied eels, burgers and plenty of other goodies. There was a bar, a stage with a band and an ice cream van parked in the driveway for the children.

It was planned for late September 2011 and by the time the date arrived we'd had RSVPs from around 200 people.

On the morning of the shindig I woke up buzzing with anticipation and was looking forward to the events ahead. There were several guests travelling from overseas who I hadn't seen for years and I was excited about catching up with them and hearing their news. It was going to be a good night! John was asleep beside me, mouth agape, snoring loudly. I nudged him awake. He had his chores to do and I wanted to make sure he did them in good time. I myself had some running around to do that day and then I got ready at home.

The night soon arrived, as did the guests. A free bar got everyone in high spirits and I watched the evening unfold with a grin on my face. I had a champagne flute in my hand for most of the night and periodically, people would wander up to me.

'Having a good night, Sal?' they'd ask. 'Getting into the swing of things?'

I was, but not in the way most people assumed. Although every now and then I'm partial to a glass of pink champagne or a decent glass of red wine, most of the time my drink of choice is ginger ale. To all intents and purposes I am teetotal; I don't drink and I haven't really done so for a good 25 years. The reason for my abstinence has been a secret up until now. Formerly a binge drinker, I used to drink so much I had to give up. I would drink to get out of my head; I was a very heavy drinker. When I was young, I used to like vodka. If I continued drinking I could easily have been a problem drinker. I would get so smashed I'd forget what I'd done and it would take me a good three days to get over a session. By then I had three children – it was not a good way to behave – but at the time I thought it was hysterical to get so drunk I'd pass out and have to be carried out of a party by John and a friend. We've all done it but I did it through my twenties and thirties. Sundays were usually wiped out. I would rouse with a stinking hangover and have to prepare a Sunday roast. Although I would go through the motions, I was dead inside. It happened every weekend because John and I loved a party. Most Saturday nights we had the parties at home because we couldn't get babysitters but whenever we could, we went to friends' houses. I didn't think there was anything unusual in getting drunk because all our friends were doing it too. The way you relaxed at the weekend was to get off your head but that didn't make it right.

I started drinking in my late teens but didn't become a habitual drinker until later in life. I still remember the first time I had a drink in a pub; I was a teenager and had been taken on a date to a pub in Putney, on the River Thames. I asked for a Campari because I'd seen an ad for it on television and so I tried to pretend I knew what I was asking for.

When the date I was with explained that I would probably need a mixer I told him no, I wanted it neat.

'You sure you don't want lemonade?' he asked.

I shook my head.

Neat, the aperitif tasted like medicine. I took one sip and screwed my face up.

'What's wrong?' my date asked.

'It tastes horrible,' I said.

After that I quickly woke up to the fact that gin and orange cordial was a much nicer drink. I loved it. Then the first time I got properly drunk was a little while later. I had an older boyfriend and it was his 21st birthday party. I drank whisky; I remember sliding down a wall. The next morning I woke up wrapped in a blanket and I'd been vomiting. After that I could never drink whisky again.

In later years, when I really started drinking properly I drank neat vodka on the rocks. I gave up after a particularly messy night. John and I had hosted a party at our house and predictably I'd got blotto. A friend rang me the following morning when I was nursing a hangover and trying to sort out the kids.

'Do you remember what you did with your bra last night?' she laughed.

'No,' I croaked. I wracked my brain but the events of the previous evening were a blank. 'I can't recall a thing.'

'Go and have a look in your cupboard under the stairs,' she said.

So I did. The upright Hoover was under the stairs and my bra was wrapped around the handle.

'What's that doing there?' I asked John absently.

He shook his head and tutted.

'You took your bra off in front of everyone last night when you doing a drunken imitation of Freddie Mercury,' he told me.

Apparently I'd tried to recreate Queen's *I Want to Break Free* video, in which Freddie is dressed as a woman vacuum cleaning. But I really couldn't remember a thing, and it frightened me.

'You do things like that every time we have a party and you get drunk,' said John. 'If I'm honest, it's not funny. It's disgusting.'

As my hangover cleared I started to wonder what I was doing to the kids: each weekend their mum was drunk. By the end of the day I resolved never to get drunk again. I stopped just like that and as the weeks went by, I really liked the feeling after a party of being in control and of waking up without a hangover. I realised that I used to be irritable; I didn't want to do things with the kids.

At my 60th people thought I'd been on the sauce and I even played up to it and pretended to be tipsy. What's really interesting is that I didn't miss it at all – I had just as much fun, if not more, and I could remember everything that happened. It was the first time ever that John made a speech that made sense! I had a lump in my throat listening to him as he told the guests how hard I worked and what a wonderful wife and mother I'd been. He was articulate and honest and when he finished, he got a standing ovation. I was filled with love and it reminded me why I'd married him in the first place. As I looked round at my husband and family, I felt both lucky and sad at the same time. My two daughters, Fern and Rebecca, were there with my four grandchildren, George, Arthur, Max and Freddie. But there was a missing part of the family: my estranged daughter Jemma and her four children, who I had not seen for many years. Out of respect for them I had not talked about the details of why they no longer spoke to me but the door was, and always is, open for them and at times such as my 60th, their absence felt like a missing limb.

The party was on a Saturday and the following day I woke early with a clear head and started to tidy up the mess that was left in the marquee. I'd never seen so many empty bottles of booze! As the rest of the family and guests rose, they came in to help and after an hour or so we had dozens of bin bags full of empties.

'There must have been some very drunk people here last night!' I laughed. We were finding bottles everywhere around the gardens. All day long the phone rang with people calling to say thank you for a wonderful night. The band had played on into the early hours and thankfully the neighbours all seemed to take it in good spirit. I cooked a roast and around ten of us sat down at a table in the marquee for lunch. The rest of the afternoon was spent lazing around as our guests left.

Everything was rosy. I'd just moved into the house of my dreams, the autumn leg of the tour was underway and bookings for the following year were looking healthy. As far as I was hearing the fourth series of *On The Road* was in the bag and there was a possibility I would be given a chat show too. I was healthy, I was thin... I was on a roll. Everything was lovely.

I was bobbing along on a calm sea.

Chapter 19
The storm breaks

I woke on Monday morning full of positivity. We had no shows booked in that day so I had planned to go into the office, which was a few miles from my home in Reigate, Surrey. I had a team of talented people there who worked for the company I had set up: Sally Morgan Enterprises. The company looked after the tour and some other businesses I was involved in. My personal manager, Hayley, was based there. She was my main link to what was going on in the office and we spent a lot of time together. We spoke several times a day and so it wasn't unusual when my phone rang first thing in the morning and Hayley's details flashed up on the caller ID screen.

I answered.

'Please don't worry, Sally,' Hayley began, 'there is a story in the *Daily Mail* today that you will need to have a look at.'

My heart sank. 'What now?' I thought.

Hayley went on to explain that the newspaper had published a story based on the ludicrous allegations made by the two anonymous callers to the local radio phone-in show in Ireland.

'How bad is it?' I asked.

'It's quite a big story,' Hayley admitted. 'And it's online.'

The *Daily Mail* had one of the most widely read websites on the planet. It dawned on me that a lot of people were going to see the story and I hadn't been given any opportunity to answer whatever it alleged against me. I told Hayley I would be in the office in a while and we would work out what to do then.

Nervously, I opened my laptop and looked at the site. The story was prominent and illustrated with a photograph of me. As I read it and felt as if I was reading about someone else, my heart started to race. I felt panic rising in my stomach. As Hayley had said, the story repeated the allegation made by the women on the radio show that two technicians working at a theatre in Ireland had relayed information to me about audience members. The inference was that somehow information had been gleaned from members of the audience prior to the show and was then being broadcast to me secretly so that I could use it in the show. I was being called a cheat.

No one from the paper had contacted the women from the radio show to verify the story, they had not contacted the theatre to confirm the details either and no one had contacted me or my office to put the allegations to me and allow me to refute them, which was unfair and as far as I was concerned, contrary to the principals of balanced journalism.

I had a sick feeling in my stomach. Crestfallen, the air had been knocked out of me. At first I couldn't take it all in. The implications were huge. I called out to John and he came into the room and started to read through the story.

'How can they do this?' I asked. Tears were beginning to prick my eyes.

'It's complete rubbish,' he said, shaking his head. 'How are they allowed to print stuff like this?'

My mind was racing. I'd been working as a medium for long enough to realise the implications of such a serious allegation. And then I started to think of the impact the story would have on my family and friends too.

'So that's how she does it,' Fern and Rebecca would be told by people who knew who their mother was; my loved ones would have to face the barrage of questions that such an accusation inevitably invites. And what about the impact on my fans? Thousands of people put their trust in me: if they read the lies and believed them that trust would be completely compromised. My work relied on a three-way triangle of trust between spirit, my fans and me. Without that mutual trusting bond, the process would not work. Spirit would not come through and I would not be able to pass on messages. Anything that chipped away at that unique interplay and put up barriers in the process could not be good. The more I thought about what was being alleged, the sadder I got.

'We need to get a statement up on my website denying this rubbish and putting the record straight,' I told John.

Not long after I read the story the phone calls started. Friends and family began getting in touch. All of them were outraged.

'I know,' I told them, 'it's a load of rubbish. There is no truth to it at all.'

Those who knew me knew the truth but it was everyone else I was worried about.

I drove to the office and there was an atmosphere of worry and indignation inside. Everyone there relied on me for their livelihoods. They were all concerned about the wider impact of what had been written. Along with the sadness, I started to feel a growing sense of anger at the injustice of what was being alleged. There was no proof whatsoever, it was all lies.

I knew I had to act but I didn't know what to do, so I sat down with John and Hayley and we started to formulate a course of action to defend my reputation. We contacted the theatre where the allegation originated. They were equally upset as by association the piece implied that they were also being dishonest and cheating the audience who had paid hard-earned money to come to the show. As I spoke to them I learned that the sound technicians who were accused of being part of the alleged ruse were sub-contracted casual staff; by association they too were accused of being cheats. So I issued a statement categorically denying the claim, as did the theatre. I also pointed out that the members of staff who were supposed to be feeding me information were, in fact, sub-contracted by the theatre and so not part of my team at all. Surely if I'd been conducting such a well-thought-out and complicated con I would have entrusted the execution of it to my own staff, rather than casual workers I did not know and had no links with.

In the face of these facts it was very obvious that the story was wrong and I mistakenly believed that would be the end of it. My team requested that the newspaper remove the allegation from its website and issue an apology. It seemed like a logical and fair course of action.

While all this was going on the phone continued to ring. Some people were calling in to offer support, while others were calling to ask whether the report was true. It was exasperating, continually defending ourselves against the allegations, and in amongst the calls from family, friends, fans and business colleagues we started to get calls from a few lawyers too.

'You can't let them get away with it. You need to defend your reputation,' was the general message. I just hoped the story would be removed and that would be the end of it. The rest of the day was spent fire-fighting, answering questions and defending myself.

Of course that wasn't the end of it. The story had gone online on one of the world's biggest websites and inevitably was picked up by other media outlets and websites. Despite the statement I had issued, by the time I went to bed that night the story had gone global. Every major newspaper in the UK was repeating it on their website. The allegation spread like an unstoppable virus and the sceptics were having a field day. Is this the proof that Psychic Sally is a cheat? they asked. Plainly it was not but by that time I was just a small voice in a growing storm. No one could hear me, and no one wanted to. Ironically, rather than look at the evidence rationally and objectively, which would have led to the obvious conclusion that the allegations were nonsense, people delighted in putting the boot in and believed what they were being fed.

My misery persisted. Two days later the same newspaper printed another story: a follow-up to the original piece. This time it was written by a well-known sceptic: the magician Paul Zenon. In the piece he discussed his views on psychics and the allegation made against me was repeated.

By that time the story was being discussed on television programmes and on radio shows. My phone was ringing off the hook. Journalists from all over the world were calling to speak to me. No matter how much I defended myself, I was not being heard. The comment sections under each story were full of invective, I was being called all sorts of names and people took to social media to attack me.

I felt crushed under the weight of a force I could not control. It was absolutely horrific. Everything I had ever done was being questioned and pulled apart. Now I began to get abusive messages through my website and on Twitter. I was accused of taking advantage of the bereaved and vulnerable.

It is fair to say that in the space of a few days in late September 2011 my world completely imploded. Up until that point I had always thought of myself as a strong person. I had weathered plenty of storms in my life and through necessity had grown a thick skin. But in the days that followed I crumbled like a wet biscuit. I felt panicky, emotionally drained and at times hopeless. It was like a crater had opened up under me, a sinkhole. Bang! I was gone, sucked into the deep. I lost motivation and I started to lose heart too.

Initially I had assumed that everyone would understand that the story wasn't true, that it was obviously a lie. Then, as the days unfolded, I couldn't understand why people continued to insist it was true. Why was no one listening to me?

Meanwhile the story continued to snowball. I heard from people in Australia because the news channels there had picked up on it.

John and I had a crisis meeting.

'We need to do something, Sally,' he said. 'It's your reputation that is being attacked. This could have really serious consequences for everything.'

It was true: theatres were beginning to worry. Ticket sales would inevitably be affected. There was an obvious and major commercial impact on the allegations but what hurt more than that was the personal attack on me the allegations constituted and the effect they were having on my fans, who were started to question whether or not I was a fake. If true, the allegations meant that all those magical moments, those hundreds of messages, all that hope I had given people was meaningless. I couldn't cope with that thought.

'I don't know what to do,' I wept.

Finally, after several days of panic and despondency, a plan was formulated after the unlikely intervention of a friend of mine. Uri Geller is a world-famous psychic. Famously he uses his powers to bend spoons. I've known Uri for years and when he heard about the story he rang me.

'You can't stand for it, Sally,' he said. 'It goes to the core of everything you are. You need to protect your reputation.'

Uri had been involved in court cases before.

'You need to sue to restore your reputation,' he advised.

I knew he was right. The newspaper had not removed the story. As long as it was out there, I would always have a cloud hanging over me. Uri gave me the details of a lawyer, who I rang. The first thing the lawyer asked was, is it true?

'Of course it isn't,' I sighed. They had to ask.

I mulled the idea over for a few days and then out of the blue another lawyer I knew through a friend contacted me to offer his services. Graham Atkins came with a personal recommendation. He had been involved in the high-profile libel case between TV presenter Anna Richardson and the Hollywood movie actor and politician Arnold

Schwarzenegger. Anna sued the California governor and two aides over comments they made about her claims that he groped her in December 2000. The action was settled out of court.

So I made up my mind.

'OK,' I said. 'We should meet up and discuss what to do.'

Graham drove over to my house immediately and we sat down and discussed the option.

I felt backed into a corner; I knew it was not going to be easy because I was going up against one of the largest and most powerful newspapers in the country. Graham warned that it would take time and money but ultimately I had to take action. It was the first time I had ever taken a stand against those accusing me of trickery and I did so because the story was destroying the trust my fans had placed in me.

Chapter 20
Courting controversy

The following months were a blur as I started to acquaint myself with the British legal system. The *Daily Mail* decided to fight the case, which meant I was in it for the long haul. We were suing for libel because the article was false and it damaged my reputation. My solicitor Graham Atkins explained that we needed a watertight case; we needed witnesses and statements to prove there was no truth whatsoever in the allegation that I had used a hidden mic during the show in Ireland.

Behind the scenes interviews and meetings took place as we worked out a plan of action. It felt good to be finally doing something but I was under no illusions. The legal process is very long, complex and expensive. We went to Ireland to speak to the two technicians who had been implicated in the story and took statements from them. Slowly we built up our case against the newspaper.

The news leaked out that I was launching a legal action and the general reaction was that I was either very brave or extremely stupid. The truth was simpler than that: I was very innocent and I had been wronged.

Up until that point I had been running on adrenaline. My fight or flight response had kicked in and

I was in defence mode. But as the months dragged on the enormity of what had been done to me and the impact it was having started to sink in. No matter how positive I was, it became hard to fight back the feelings of hopelessness which threatened to overwhelm me.

In his call to me Uri Geller had touched on the crux of the matter: the article had questioned who I was as a person. It implied that I was a fake. I could not remember a day when I wasn't aware of my gift – I didn't just *do* mediumship, I *was* a medium. My whole identity and life was built around the fact that I was psychic and that as a result I could do things people found amazing. If it were true, if I was a fake, what did that mean about my whole life? That it had all been a lie and I'd been lying to myself, my loved ones and those who trusted in me since I could remember? The thought bored into me like a maggot eating into an apple. And it started to rot inside me. It became a doubt. Was I a cheat? Was the article correct? The logical part of me knew it wasn't true but I was coming under such intense criticism from every corner that it started to do funny things with my head. Everywhere I went, I felt the need to defend myself. I became preoccupied with what others were thinking about me.

During those months my professional life carried on as best it could and I had meetings and did shows but whenever I was talking to people I was always trying to work out what they were thinking. Often no one mentioned the piece but still I tortured myself.

Did they think I was a cheat? Did they believe I was psychic? It was the elephant in the room.

To make matters worse, because there was an active legal case I couldn't talk about it during the shows. I couldn't go on TV and defend myself; I had to keep my mouth shut while everyone else was free to discuss and debate whether or not I was a cheat. For months and months I was asked to do interviews but had to fend off the requests.

The chatter and vitriol continued online. There were Tweets, Facebook posts, blogs and forums. My website was regularly used as a message board on which people posted hate mail. All kinds of cranks and oddballs came out of the woodwork to join in the tirade. Mostly I put a brave face on things and tried to brush the comments off, but one letter really affected me deeply. It came from an old client of mine. I had seen her for many years, back in the days before I started touring. I'd helped her through some very dark years following the death of her husband and we had formed a bond, which crossed over from a professional relationship to one of friendship. I was very fond of her and she had found great comfort in the messages I could pass to her. I'd told her so many things that I could not possibly have known without the ability to contact the spirit world and she trusted in my ability. I had given her hope and nursed her through the terrible grief and loss she had suffered. The letter she sent called all that into doubt.

'I am so sad to read that it was all a trick, Sally,'

she wrote. 'I trusted you and I feel betrayed. How could you do that to me and all the other people who believed in you?' As I read those words I felt numb. At each word another piece of my broken heart fell away. I wanted to hug her and tell her it was all a lie and that I would never, ever cheat the people who came to me.

The drip-drip effect of all the negativity just fed the doubt; it was insidious. I tried to stop it by recalling some of the countless incidents from my past that could not be explained away by any trickery. At eight years old I told one of my teachers that I knew he had thrown crockery at his wife that morning. And he had. How did I know that? Was I cheating then? How did I know the names of the dead relatives of the people I was talking to even when I was a teenager? There were no hidden earpieces then. In the early days of my practice at home there was no Google or Facebook either. I couldn't check the social media profiles of those who were coming to see me but somehow once they sat with me I managed to know intimate details about their lives.

I'd even started to change the way I behaved on stage. At first I did not realise it and then one of the crew pointed it out.

'Every time you start talking to someone who has stood to take a message you ask them to confirm that you have never met them before.'

He was right – I caught myself doing it again and again.

'I don't know you, do I?' I would ask repeatedly at every show. 'There is no way I could have known what I have just told you, is there?'

All the time I double-checked myself. I was so aware that people in the audience might have read the stories or that there could be people there who had bought tickets with the sole aim of catching me out that I was constantly letting them know there was no trickery involved. It felt like I was walking on eggshells. Thankfully my ability never left me and I continued to work as I'd always done: with faith and belief. And because of that, spirit never deserted me.

I was paranoid; I found it very hard to trust people.

The months rumbled on slowly as my legal team worked hard to get an apology and to clear my name. All the time my friends and family had to endure constant remarks from people. At best they had to bat back questions about the claims, at worst they were forced to endure taunts and abuse. It was their support and the support and strength I got from my fans that kept me going and ultimately kept me sane.

The first six months were the worst. At one point I seriously considered giving it all up and leaving the country. It was one night after a show. I was with John and we were heading home in the car.

'You're quiet,' he said to me. 'What's troubling you?'

As ever the show had been a success but the

magic events on stage only held off the black feeling that returned whenever I was on my own and at the mercy of my own thoughts. I turned to him.

'I think I've had enough of it all, John,' I sighed. 'I don't know if I can carry on doing this. I am tired.'

'What do you mean?' he asked. 'Tired of what?'

'I'm tired of having to defend myself and feeling like I am living under a cloud. Our lives are in limbo while all this is going on. I just want it to end or to go away. I think we should sell up and move away. Start again somewhere else, emigrate.'

The roles of our relationship had reversed. I was always the positive one, my glass was always half full. John, on the other hand, was usually Mr Doom and Gloom. If a negative could be had from a situation he would find it – it's why we work so well together. He is the yin to my yang! In this instance he gave me a pep talk.

'You can't think like that, Sally. What has happened is unfair and it is all lies, we know that and the rest of the world will know that too. If you leave now and give up, some people will take that as a sign that the story is true. We have no choice but to see this thing through, get justice and be strong. We have nothing to hide. Things will get better, I promise.'

But a very dark cloud descended over me for 18 months. I went to Hell and I stayed there for a long time. And in my darkest hours I thought about ending it all. For the first time in my life I thought, 'I've got to die, my family can't see this.' Everyone would be better off if I wasn't there, I thought. I just couldn't shift the black cloud and so I started to think seriously about ending my life with pills. Absent-mindedly I wondered what the best ones would be and how many I'd need. I knew there was an afterlife and I knew how beautiful and peaceful it was. Simply by crossing over to the other side I could put a stop to this misery. I went into a downward spiral and as I was falling, I was so confused and all my drive disappeared; it was horrific. Two things kept me from doing the unimaginable. Even when I was overwhelmed by dark thoughts, at the back of my mind I had so many memories of readings I had done for bereaved people whose loved ones had taken their own lives. Suicide was perhaps the hardest form of passing for those left behind. The emotions it left crushed people; it left doubt, guilt and anger. I couldn't do that to the people I loved. The second thing that stopped me was John. He could see how hopeless I was becoming and it frightened him. One day I didn't want to get out of bed – I lay there with the curtains pulled, I had no energy at all. I just wanted to disappear. John was really scared. He tried his best to lift my spirits but he didn't know what to do. He's not very tactile. Only in our very private moments does he show his emotions but he came up and held my hand and stroked it. I was exhausted, emotionally and physically. John held me.

'You have to get up, you can't go on like this,' he said gently. He had tears in his eyes. I looked into them and I saw that glimmer of his fear and it brought me round, like someone had smashed me in the chest. I realised that I needed to fight.

I squeezed John's hand.

'If we have to sell the house we will clear my name,' I said through gritted teeth.

After that I continued to face the onslaught of abuse with as much resolve as I could muster. I had people calling me a fat whore and even calling for me to be beheaded. There were death threats. I felt terrified and besieged.

One day my phone rang. I didn't recognise the number so I answered tentatively.

The voice at the other end of the line was coarse and aggressive. It was a woman with an Irish accent and she spewed out hate-filled abuse and threats before ringing off. I stood there in my kitchen, shaking.

By the time I had composed myself the phone rang again.

'Who is this?' I said as the woman continued her tirade. 'How *dare* you call me! How did you get this number?'

Again she hung up.

When she called a third time I didn't answer. Throughout the day the calls kept coming. I ignored them but each time the woman left abusive messages.

Later that day Hayley called to tell me the office had received abusive calls too. It also coincided with several abusive emails and messages on my website. I hoped that, like many of the other trolls, she would get bored and go away but it worried me. How on earth did she get my number and if she had that, did she know where I lived?

But the messages didn't stop; they got worse. Over the following days they continued and the woman started to make death threats. Terrified, I called the police, who took it very seriously. The CID became involved and came round and took statements. They traced the number and the IP addresses of where the emails were being sent from. The calls were coming from Ireland and officers from Surrey got in touch with the Garda in Ireland, who visited the woman and questioned her. They discovered she had worked for a department store I used in London and had got my details from a private database. Then they asked if I wanted to press charges. I didn't have the energy to cope with a second court case. The woman was cautioned but as a precaution I had CCTV put up around the house.

Throughout the time all this was going on I tried my best to put on a brave face and continued to tour. Often I found solace on stage; I drew strength from it. When I was on stage in front of an audience no one could hurt me. I could shut out all the other stuff and immerse myself in the spirit world. It was hugely comforting. I was still able to help people and share hope with them. And I felt that I was supported by the spirit world too: the energy that I tapped into was an energy of love and positivity and I came away from each show feeling calm and relaxed. I think, in their own special way, the spirits I interacted with were helping me along. Intuitive entities, they hone in on our emotions and they could sense the turmoil in me and did what they could to help.

For 18 months we made a case and built our defence. My resolve increased throughout the period. You get to a stage in a defamation case when each side has to show the other what evidence they have: our case was watertight. I had got to the stage where the critics and the cynics had made me so strong that I didn't care if I lost it all.

I knew I was innocent and I wasn't about to let them get away with it.

Chapter 21
The wizard of Oz

Before the *Daily Mail* article was published we had planned a family trip to Australia. I thought about cancelling it. As far as I was concerned Christmas was cancelled that year. How could I celebrate with such a weight on my shoulders? But I knew that would be selfish. Everyone had been looking forward to the trip and it would not have been fair if I'd pulled out at the last minute.

'Come on,' said John. 'It will take your mind off things.'

I also had a deeper concern; a niggling insecurity that once I arrived in Australia the criticism would continue. I knew that there was interest in my work and me on the other side of the world. The first three series of *On The Road* had such an appeal that the programme makers were able to sell the shows in other countries and one of the territories broadcasting them was Australia. They were doubly interested in me there because of my links with Princess Diana, which is why in the aftermath of the *Daily Mail* story reports of it were published in Australia.

If I wanted to go somewhere no one knew me, I was heading to the wrong corner of the globe. I would be better off heading for the Amazon jungle!

We planned to stay in Australia for several weeks and travel throughout the vast country. We had several friends there with whom we had arranged to stay and I didn't want to let them down either. In December 2011, half-broken and fragile, I boarded the plane along with the rest of my family and headed off on the two-day journey. We had a short stopover in Dubai and arrived in Perth, tired and jet-lagged.

The flight had allowed me plenty of time to think, which wasn't healthy given my state of mind. I tried to distract myself with movies on the in-flight entertainment system but it was no good. Stuck in an airplane cabin with nowhere to go my mind kept coming back to the problems I was facing and the long road ahead. By the time I disembarked I was questioning whether I had done the right thing. I felt trapped. There I was on the other side of the world and if things got too bad for me there was no way I could turn around and go home; it wasn't as if I could hop in a cab.

Walking through the airport I kept my sun-glasses on and my head down. Then I felt eyes boring into me.

A shout made me jump.

'Sally Morgan!'

I kept my head down.

'It is you, isn't it?' It was a woman's voice with an Australian accent. I began walking faster and heard footsteps following me. My heart started beating. I braced myself for the inevitable abuse.

'Hold up, Sally!'

People were beginning to look around. I didn't want to get chased through the airport so I stopped and gritted my teeth. As I turned round I was met by a grinning, friendly face, a little red and a little breathless.

'Strewth!' she exclaimed in true Ozzie fashion. 'You don't 'arf move fast for a little 'un!'

I couldn't help but smile.

'I thought it was you!' she continued. 'I love your show, Sally. Can I have a picture with you?'

But the abuse never came: the lady was lovely, a real fan who didn't mention the story.

'I've seen all your shows,' she gushed. 'I think you are amazing!'

I happily posed for a photo while the rest of the family raised their eyebrows and waited. The woman wished me luck and left. She was the first of many people who recognised me and who showed nothing but openness and good spirit. If the story was ever mentioned then it was always followed by a declaration of support.

'Don't let the buggers get you down!' was a refrain I heard repeatedly over those weeks.

As a family we went all over Australia; we went from Perth to Adelaide and Sydney and then right up to Port Douglas. We almost did a lap of the entire country and visited some amazing places. It was lovely to spend so much quality time with my loved ones. I'd been so busy and preoccupied with touring over the preceding years that I had almost forgotten how lucky I was to have such a wonderful family. There was no drama and whenever I was recognised I got a really warm welcome.

Everyone was so friendly and open. Whenever I mentioned to strangers what I did for a living far from being sceptical and questioning me, they were fascinated. Even on television psychics were accepted. In the UK there are rulings: broadcasters have to make disclaimers before they transmit psychic shows to tell the audience that the shows are for entertainment purposes only. It always struck me as strange. They do not have to put disclaimers on before *Songs of Praise*. In Australia there was none of that.

Whenever a psychic goes on television in the UK, there will inevitably be a sceptic there to argue against them. As a consequence, whenever I went on TV shows in the UK, especially chat shows, I felt I had to defend myself. Everyone else got to go on and talk about their new show or their new book, psychics had to go on and convince people they were genuine, usually to a hostile host who would be raising an eyebrow. It was never a level playing field. But none of that seemed to be happening in Australia; everyone was perfectly accepting and interested. I started to formulate an idea. One night in Adelaide I spoke to John about it.

'What would you think about coming out here for longer?' I asked.

'What, to live?'

'No, to work,' I said.

John thought about it.

'Maybe,' he eventually said. 'But it's a long way to come. You'd have to do more than a few dates, it's a big country.'

'What about if we started small, in little venues and then saw how things progressed? It just seems like such a friendly place. I reckon I could make a go of it.'

'Let's look into it when we get home,' suggested John.

For the rest of the holiday I was excited by the possibility that perhaps I could add a new country to my tour route. It seemed like a logical step. I was well established in the UK. Perhaps it was time to spread my wings.

I left Australia full of optimism. The time I had spent there had shown me that there was hope and there was a future; it reaffirmed my faith in my work. When I got back home I threw myself into my work. It was winter in the UK and it didn't take long for the cold and the grey to start nibbling away at my positivity. Again, I found solace on stage. Inevitably the allegation that continued to dog me had an effect on me, mentally, physically and financially. The fourth series of *On The Road* never materialised. It was impossible for the production company to commit before I had cleared my name. Until then I was damaged goods. If I stopped and thought about the unfairness of it all for too long I would get angry. Without a TV show, ticket sales for the shows were inevitably affected but my lovely fans still believed and continued to come out and see me.

I did have one bit of unexpected television work in 2012, which turned out to be a lot of fun, though. At the start of the autumn I received a call from the makers of the Channel 4 show, *Come Dine With Me*. They were making a Halloween special and they wanted me to be one of the contributors. 'Why not?' I thought. I loved cooking and had always enjoyed hosting parties so I jumped at the chance.

The programme format is a competition: there are four hosts and each one invites the other three to their house, where they throw a dinner party and offer some entertainment. Everyone marked each other on the standard of the food and the atmosphere. I'd watched the programme many times before and often it seemed to me all you had to do was get the other guests smashed to win, but I wanted to be a bit more subtle than that. As it was Halloween-themed I was keen to add plenty of other touches to make for a memorable night.

The idea was to concoct a three-course meal. I started to plan a feast. For the first course I thought I'd do shellfish. I planned to cook langoustines, which are like a cross between a prawn and a tiny lobster. I would cover them with a fake blood sauce. And then I had a brainwave.

'Do you reckon you can buy tiny prawn-sized coffins?' I asked Fern one night.

'What on earth for?' she said.

'For the *Come Dine With Me* starter.'

She shrugged and started looking online. Eventually she found some, which just goes to prove that if you can think of it, it's available to buy online. We ordered them and I had my starter: Prawn of the Dead!

As the day of filming approached I began to get more competitive. What started out as a quirky dinner party for four turned into a full-blown production. I had a friend who owned his own undertakers so I called him one day.

'Do you mind if I borrow a coffin?'

He didn't, and so on the night I had a prop.

Fern called in a favour from a friend who ran her own dance school: we needed zombies and she supplied them.

On the night the guests arrived at my house they turned out to be Katie Price's ex-husband Alex Reid, former glamour model Nicola McLean and Robert Englund, who played Freddy Krueger in the *Nightmare on Elm Street* movies. Each of them was lovely. Alex, who was famed for dressing in a corset and suspenders and calling himself Roxanne, received plenty of well-meaning mickey-taking. Bless him, he wasn't the sharpest tool in the box.

My guests were greeted by several zombies wandering around the grounds ominously. The dance school had done an amazing job with the make-up and even I found it a bit creepy. They all got totally into character and at one stage one of the 'actors' – a 14-year-old girl who looked like a ghost – rapped on the window behind Nicola McLean, who nearly jumped out of her skin. When everyone turned to look the opening bars of Michael Jackson's 'Thriller' blared out from a sound system that had been set up outside. The zombies sprang to life and did a perfectly executed dance, just like in the original video. It was priceless (just like Alex!). I loved every minute of it and at the end of the process the other hosts voted me the winner, which was a lovely end to it all.

Meanwhile, my office had been looking at the logistics of booking dates for me in Australia. After a bit of careful research it appeared that there was a demand for a travelling psychic over in Oz – they didn't care about the allegations. We started booking venues and tickets went on sale. I was going international! All I had to do now was sort out the small matter of a rather large legal case.

Chapter 22
Victory

As the months moved on I immersed myself in work. The allegations had the effect of making me look closely at what I did and I began to analyse the processes that took place each night when I stood on stage. I tried to look at my work scientifically to see if there were patterns. More than ever I started to think harder about what I was doing before I became fascinated by the psychic process; I looked for patterns and clues, anything that would provide some indication about the how and the why. Although confident of victory in the case, I knew that I was being questioned. There was a possibility I would be called to give evidence and in those circumstances I would have to stand before the judge and explain my work.

Over the years so many people had asked me what goes on inside my head and I wanted to know too; I wanted to look at my psychic ability and analyse myself. Since I was not an academic I was not able to use scientific experience. The only test I ever passed in life was my driving test and I didn't pass that the first time! But I was curious so I set out to question everything and to find the kernels of truth about what it meant to be a medium and how it all worked.

The more I thought about it, the more I realised there was a pattern – messages always seemed to follow a theme. There were so many memorable shows during which one message linked to another; they were strung together like pearl necklaces. For example, at a show in East Anglia the energy from the first message was very intense. As I was introducing myself, I felt confused; my head was muddled. The message was from a young man. His spirit was showing me what he was feeling in the hours before his death. I felt overwhelmed. The spirit showed me an image of him running around, holding his head in his hands. I relayed this to the audience and a young woman stood up to take the message. While she was talking a woman in spirit showed herself and mouthed the number 67. I asked the lady in the audience what the significance was and she said it was the number of her dead gran's house.

'Your nan is here for you,' I said.

Other spirits showed themselves. The next gave me the name Dan and said the word 'justice'. A woman directly in front of the first lady stood up and took the message. She mentioned that she knew a man called Dan in spirit, who had died as a result of medical negligence.

As I was talking to the woman, the spirit of a man appeared to the side of me. He walked into view and he was holding two baby boys. I knew instinctively they were twins. The name Andrew popped into my head. He wanted someone in the audience to know that the twins were at peace. In the same small area of the theatre another woman stood up.

'My mum had twin boys and when they were six weeks old, they died in their sleep,' she explained. 'They were found dead in their cot, one at one end, one at the other. One was called Andrew and the other was Daniel.'

The audience cheered.

'That's the link,' I explained. 'That's the hook from the previous message. Your dad is in spirit and he is there, holding the babies.'

The woman nodded. Messages led seamlessly into each other as spirits lined up to piggyback off the energy of the message before.

'What we've got here is a little pocket of energy at the back of the theatre,' I explained. 'I don't control the messages, they control me.'

It was incidents such as these that convinced me that there was some sort of plan going on. Everything was orchestrated. I lost count of the number of shows I did where messages seemed to concentrate on pockets in the audience. One person would take a message then the next set of messages would be taken by people sitting a few seats away. Often it turned out that random audience members sitting close to each other had things in common. I began to get the feeling that spirit was controlling everything; we were all puppets and the spirits were pulling the strings in ways I would never comprehend. They made amazing things happen.

While I wondered at the supernatural marvels that were happening in my professional life the more mundane process of my defamation action plodded through the courts. There were a lot of behind-the-scenes negotiations between lawyers. My legal team had all its ducks in a row so I put my faith in the legal system. I knew categorically that the allegations were false and so I couldn't see how the case could fail. Stranger things have happened, however, so throughout the process I still had to fight the niggling worry that somehow a judge would look unfavourably on me. I had visions of myself standing up in court and having to prove that there is an afterlife. It would have been the most explosive trial of the century. God – whatever you take Him, Her or It to be – would be on trial.

The criticisms continued to be directed against me. Thankfully the really nasty stuff had died down. By the spring of 2013 it had been 18 months since the allegations were first made and although they were still there on the Internet, people had thankfully forgotten. I was yesterday's news and that was exactly how I wanted to remain.

At the end of the spring my lawyers and the legal team came to an agreement. The *Daily Mail* conceded it could not prove that the story was true and so accepted that it was false. It agreed to pay damages and costs. When my lawyer Graham Atkins called to tell me the news I almost fainted. A wave of emotion swept over me. I was ecstatic and relieved but also sad and angry that I had been put through so much in the first place. No amount of compensation would cover the emotional distress. And the whole process had been long, drawn-out and costly. Even though the legal costs would be paid, the rules stipulated that our whole costs would not be repaid, just a percentage. I kept asking myself why hadn't they simply taken the story down and printed an apology?

Over the following weeks the lawyers thrashed out a deal. The newspaper was to print an apology and would also make a statement in the open court.

In June 2013 I found myself finally at the end of a long road. The statement was to be read out at the High Court in London. The courtroom was much smaller than I had expected; hard wooden benches were set out in formal rows, like pews in a church. They faced forward and were sloped towards the judge's chair, giving spectators a view of the raised seat where the decisions were made. Around the side of the chamber the walls were lined with dark oak panelling and bookshelves heaving under the weight of hundreds of thick, leather-bound tomes. The general impression was a cross between *Hogwarts* and *Rumpole of the Bailey*. Sombre, almost oppressive, the weight of history and authority bore down on the rows of people seated in the room. A musty smell added to the serious ambience. It was the sort of place that made you whisper and my psychic antenna was twitching; I could feel the energy seeping from the walls. All the emotions had permeated the air in that space over hundreds of years, the jubilation and the disappointments.

I had invited a few close friends and family along for support. There were also some reporters there as the case was big news. Not many people take newspapers to court for libel and win, especially psychics. At the time I failed to grasp the full impact of what I'd done – I was just glad it was over – but it was a big deal.

We met in a cafe across the road from the imposing court buildings and I tried to hide my nerves by cracking jokes and generally messing around. Graham Atkins was there, along with the QC we had used, a man called David Sherborne. The statement was being read out at 10am. At 9.45am I looked at the clock and took a deep breath.

'Let's get this over and done with and move on with our lives,' I told John. We walked over the road as a group and passed through the security at the front of the building. The courtroom we had been assigned was on the first floor, up a narrow staircase. One by one we filed in through a heavy wooden door.

Inside, I sat down and looked around me. I was surrounded by scores of friends and family; my supporters and loved ones. They were waiting quietly in anticipation, speaking occasionally in hushed voices. Every now and then someone would catch my eye and give me an encouraging smile or a wink.

The black-robed judge took his seat. John was sitting next to me and squeezed my hand. I smiled back at him. Meanwhile my heart was pounding in my chest.

Graham Atkins was dressed in his black robes and looked very serious indeed when he stood and began reading the statement that had been agreed by the legal team representing the newspaper.

'Mrs Morgan is a psychic. In the last five years or so, she has become well-known through appearing on television and through her theatre shows around the country, in which she performs to large audiences. She has performed in over 600 shows in more than 100 different theatres or venues, to audiences stretching into the hundreds of thousands.'

He went on to explain the basis of why I was suing the newspaper for libel. I clung onto every word.

'The allegation contained in the article that Mrs Morgan cheated the audience in Dublin is completely false and defamatory of her. It has also caused enormous distress to Mrs Morgan, who decided, given the newspaper's initial defence of the article, that she had no choice but to commence legal proceedings against the publisher of the *Daily Mail*. I am pleased to say that the *Daily Mail* has now accepted that the allegation is untrue and is here by its solicitor today to apologise for the publication of the allegation. It has also agreed to pay Mrs Morgan substantial damages, together with her legal costs.'

Then the newspaper's solicitor stood to make the statement.

'The *Daily Mail* withdraws the suggestion that Mrs Morgan used a secret earpiece at her Dublin show in September 2011 to receive messages from off-stage, thereby cheating her audience, which it accepts is untrue.'

I felt the weight of the last few months begin to lift from my shoulders.

'It apologises unreservedly to Mrs Morgan for publishing the allegation,' the solicitor continued.

Words had never sounded sweeter. It had been a long, hard battle but that short sentence made it all worth it. Finally, I was vindicated. I allowed myself a smile.

The judge closed the proceedings and we all filed out of the room. Just as I'd felt after my surgery a great weight had been lifted from me, a weight that had been bearing down on me for a long time.

Outside the court building a photographer took pictures. I couldn't help smiling. We went to a nearby hotel to celebrate and before long, newspapers and radio stations began calling for interviews. I spoke to one radio station, one newspaper and one magazine. I felt that it would be inappropriate to do lots and lots of interviews. Besides I didn't need to – word spread quickly. Within an hour the first reports of my victory had appeared online. The BBC reported first and, just as the offending story had spread around the world like a virus, the antidote – the story of my court victory – started to spread too.

They say mud sticks and to a large degree that is true, especially in the Internet age when stories and information get picked up and passed on through hundreds and hundreds of different websites. And once they are on those sites, they stay there unless someone takes them down. The damaging story was indeed like an infection. Traces of it could be found everywhere, even though it had been proved a lie. The following months were just as much of a headache as my team contacted as many organisations, news outlets, websites and bloggers as possible who had all published the story to let them know that it was libellous. Though time-consuming and costly, I had the law on my side and I felt that it was not fair for those lies to continue to be propagated.

In the modern age stories take on a life of their own; they may well be initially published in ignorance and without malice but I had learnt that there are corners of the Internet inhabited by fanatics and evil people who latched onto information, took it as gospel without checking facts and then used it as a rod to beat people with. They hid in the dark, behind anonymous usernames. No wonder they were called trolls. I hoped I'd never have to deal with them again.

Chapter 23
Psychic international

A few weeks after the drama of the case John and I got in a taxi and were driven to Gatwick Airport, where we boarded a plane bound for Australia. I settled back in my seat as we sped down the runway and lifted off into the blue sky. The miles dropped away and as they did so, I could feel myself start to relax. The further away from the UK we got, the further away the last two years felt. My shoulders dropped and I sank back into my seat as the jet flew out over the South Coast and across to Europe. I had done what I set out to do; I had cleared my name.

It was going to be a long flight and so I closed my eyes and let peaceful sleep drift over me. I was on my way to Australia for a series of shows. It was a new beginning for me and it couldn't have come at a better time. I'd never toured extensively in a foreign country and it felt right to put some distance between the UK and myself. Besides Australia offered something new. But I hadn't planned for the tour to coincide with the end of my legal case, I believe that was the way spirit orchestrated it.

I must have been exhausted because I slept for most of the first stage of the flight. The tour was going to be gruelling. We had booked in as many dates as we could over a five-week period covering most of the large cities in the country. The distances between each one were vast and I would be spending a lot travelling on the road and in the air. But I didn't care: for me it was a chance to test new waters and to introduce the wonders of mediumship in a new country. Excited but nervous, I hadn't felt that kind of anticipation and expectation in a while and I liked the way it felt – it was new. People laughed when I told them I liked the unexpected.

'But you are psychic, you know everything, you can see into the future,' they'd protest.

And it was true. I saw and sensed things others did not, but when it came to me and my path in life those 'knowings' as I called them remained shrouded in mist. My own destiny was an area I was not permitted to stray into. I always sensed that if I turned my gift inwards I would be breaking some kind of unwritten agreement with the spirit world. My ability was not given to me for my own benefit and to use it in such a way would be wrong. Who would want to know how things pan out anyway? I'd hate to know when I'm going to die or what will happen in between, it would be like reading the last page of amazing book; you'd spoil the story. So when we touched down after the long flight I was full of trepidation.

The reception I got was warm and welcoming. People were genuinely interested in my work and the venues started to fill up as locals and ex-pats alike began to buy tickets to find out who this strange woman from the UK, who claimed she could talk to the dead, was. And that's when I began to notice the energy: the more shows I did, the purer the psychic energy felt. I couldn't quite put my finger on it at first but then it started to make sense. The country was open; it felt like it accepted me and who I was. Sure, there were people who would raise an eyebrow and question whether I was for real but those who took the attitude of 'OK, let's see what you can do' far outnumbered the sceptics, who were adamant I was a fake and dismissed me out of hand. Even the cynics were willing to listen with an open mind. I found it very refreshing and it affected the quality of the shows. People started to trust and the more they started to trust, the more hits came through; some amazing things happened too.

In a place called Bankstown, a suburb of south-west Sydney, I sensed the spirit of a young girl. As her image materialised in my mind's eye my blood ran cold. She was stooped over and her face was directed away from me but even from my obscured viewpoint I could see the burns all over her body. I got the name Connie.

'I'm looking at something that isn't very nice,' I told the audience. 'Normally, when I have something heavy, I prefer to deal with it in the second half.' It was early in the show and I usually like to ease people in gently! But Connie would not go away.

'Her name is Connie, there were very bad burns on her. Her hair and neck area were on fire.'

I could hear the noise of something popping. Then I felt the sensation of falling from a great height. The energy felt so strong, I knew the message was meant for someone. I also got the name Ginger.

A lady took the message and explained that she had a friend who was recently murdered and her body had been set alight. But the names did not match. As much as I would have liked to give her the message, I knew it wasn't for her: the details did not match. I sensed that when Connie died there were other people present. Sadly no one else took the message and so I moved on.

Then in the interval something strange happened. Two girls approached one of my staff in the foyer and told her that a year ago there had been a house fire, a few blocks away from the theatre. Two girls had died in it; their names were Connie and Ginger. The girls said they didn't take the message because they assumed it was meant for someone else. I heard about this just before I took to the stage for the second half of the show. I could have mentioned it but I chose not to do so for two reasons. Firstly, once the message has gone, it has gone. Connie's spirit had left. I do not force spirit through and I wasn't prepared to try. That's why I am always so adamant about people taking messages – you only get one shot and it is such a rare privilege. The second reason I decided to stay silent had much to do with the battering I had received over the newspaper articles. I simply didn't want people to think that I had gone off at the interval and googled details about local tragedies.

At every show there were streams of amazing messages. A few days later I was on stage in a place called Penrith in New South Wales when another young girl came through. I could feel her and the panic she felt at the end of her life. Aged 11 when she died, she was saying what sounded like 'Orla' and I could feel that there had been something wrong with her arms.

I tried to work out what was wrong with her arms. It felt as though they were being pulled back and they felt heavy. Perhaps they had been in plaster? Then I felt water rising up. As the details were coming through I recounted them to the audience and a lady sitting near the back raised her arm.

'I don't like what I am seeing. Was she caught under her right arm? Was that how she died?'

The voice in my head became clearer.

'I think she is saying "all over",' I explained.

The lady stood.

'It's not a nice story,' she explained. 'She was raped and murdered and put in a pond with rocks in her backpack.'

Her arms were being pulled back by the weight of the rocks drawing her down.

'When she was put in that pond she was dead,' I explained. 'She is safe now.'

Show after show, the spirits came flooding through

with amazingly accurate information. At another show in a venue called The Juniors in Kingsford, New South Wales I picked up the energy of a man before I went on stage. I was sitting quietly in my dressing room when he hijacked my thoughts. The words in my mind were foreign: 'Givan... Givan...'

I also felt there had been a birth in the family.

I explained this to the audience and pointed out where in the audience he was looking. A lady stood immediately with a younger woman. I had been pointing directly at them.

'What have I said that makes sense to you?' I asked.

'My name is Givan, my father has passed away and my daughter has had a little baby girl,' she explained.

At this the audience cheered (the Aussies were very enthusiastic).

'He's not talking English,' I noted. The lady nodded.

The man in spirit showed me a scene of the baby in a lovely frilly dress and gave me the name Chris. I told the woman and tearfully she explained that her daughter's name was Christine.

'He's been there with them,' I explained.

The man went on to explain that Christine should be careful of her back and also that his daughter Rose should be careful of her head. He was keeping an eye on them from spirit. The energy was linked and I felt locked into the message. I ended the message and the ladies sat down.

The next spirit came through immediately. His

name was Steve and he had died in an accident. There had been a huge compensation claim connected to his death. The same lady stood again.

'My cousin was Steve and he died when he was hit by a train. His family were awarded compensation for it.'

It was an amazing double! The energy from the first spirit was so strong it had hooked in Steve's spirit as well.

As the tour progressed I could feel my confidence coming back to me. And the more confident I was, the more messages I passed on. It was an amazing five weeks but perhaps the high point was when I was invited on a national television show to talk about my work.

I won't lie, I was a little concerned at first – I had appeared on shows in the UK before and been hijacked by sceptical attitudes. The show in Australia was called *The Daily Edition*. I settled into my seat ready to be interviewed by host Tom Williams but as soon as he introduced himself I felt at ease because I could tell he had no other agenda than to find out about me.

He was curious but he was open and because of that I started to pick up information about him. For a moment I was confused: spirit was showing me something that I knew was a closely guarded secret. Was I supposed to say something?

Then Tom gave me the opportunity.

'Are you picking up anything about the presenters?' he asked.

I took a breath, convinced that what I was about to say was the truth but if he denied it, I would look a fool, and worse, a liar.

'There is a child on the way to you.'

Tom was dumbstruck, while his co-presenters looked on mutely as he confirmed that his wife was expecting. He explained to his emotional colleagues that he was going to break the news later in the week and that he and his wife had been trying for quite a while as most of the other people on the show had children and he was beginning to feel left out.

Everyone in the studio was emotional and it became even more amazing when I told Tom's co-host, Sally Obermeder, that she would adopt a child in the future. She explained that she had survived cancer and that made it risky for her to conceive so she had been discussing adoption.

The show was live and by the following day the news of my accuracy had spread across Australia and subsequently the world over. In a weird stroke of irony, one of the news outlets in the UK that covered the story was none other than the *Daily Mail*!

Australia was cleansing for me: all the worries and fears I had were washed away and when I returned to the UK I was physically tired from all the travelling but mentally and spiritually reinvigorated. The spirits had been there when I needed it most. They were literally swarming around me at each venue, making sure that word of my genuine ability got out.

In the months that followed things began to look up for me back home too. With the cloud of suspicion lifted, a television production company got in touch with me. One of the *On The Road* producers had started her own business and she had been talking to a network about another series. She called me and asked if I would be interested and explained that the series would be the same format as before, mixing footage from theatre shows with reality footage of John and me going about our daily lives. Of course I was I interested, I told her.

Things were looking up.

Chapter 24
Out of the frying pan...

It was July 2013 and the nation was celebrating a new arrival. George Alexander Louis, or His Royal Highness Prince George of Cambridge, to give him his full title, was the firstborn son of the Duke and Duchess of Cambridge, William and Catherine. I was over the moon for the royal couple. Misty-eyed, I'd watched on TV when the lovebirds tied the knot in 2011 and now it was beautiful to see them start a family together.

I was in Australia touring when the royal birth took place. As I watched the news reports I wished the young couple all the luck in the world. They looked so happy and Wills especially seemed so proud of his son. The baby was born with such a huge weight of expectation on his tiny shoulders. Third in line to the throne, it was strange to think that small bundle of joy would most probably one day be the King of England.

I knew that George's grandmother was looking down on him and sending him love. It was no secret that Diana had always wanted her boys, William and Harry, to lead as normal a life as possible under the circumstances. She tried very hard to bring them up as rounded human beings, which was not easy given the life of privilege they were born into. After she died in August 1997 her wish was carried out and both boys have grown into wonderful, caring men, who have inherited the common touch that made their mother so loved. She would have been so proud of William. As second in line to the throne he has had more pressure on him than his younger brother and at times has struggled with the weight of expectation that must bear down on him heavily. It's no secret that he longs to live a private life and the sad fact is it will be very hard for him to live out of the public gaze if, and when, he becomes King.

To see him cradle his newborn son was emotional. I know how much those boys meant to Diana and I know how worried she was about the complexities they would face as they grew up in the royal household. And I know how stifling royal life can be. Diana found it almost unbearable at times. There are factions and schisms within the royal household; there are people with vested interests and with their own agendas; back-biting and skulduggery.

I was always a monarchist and a royalist. I knew how Diana had struggled with royal life but the institution of the royal family is something to be proud of. The Queen has done an amazing job. Since her Coronation when she took her vows at Westminster Abbey in 1953 she has given her life to her country. It cannot be easy, knowing you will never live a normal life and that every move you make will be scrutinised, and she has carried out her duties as monarch with good grace and fortitude, even in times when her family has lurched from one crisis to the next. I'm sure there have been plenty of times when she must have held her head in her hands. The royal family has seen more than its fair share of cads and controversial characters for the last few decades.

Indeed I came face to face with one such bounder during one of my shows. As part of *Star Psychic* the programme makers arranged for me to give readings to celebrities and public figures. I was never warned who it was I would meet until the last minute. One day I was driven into the countryside outside London and told I would be going clay pigeon shooting with a famous person. When we arrived at the shooting range I immediately recognised the day's subject as he came towards me. His floppy ginger hair and self-assured swagger were the unmistakable trademarks of posh cad James Hewitt, the man made famous for having an affair with Diana, Princess of Wales.

The producer knew my history as the Princess's psychic and asked if I still wanted to do the reading. I told him I did. Now I will not divulge when Diana told me about her former lover but she did talk about him on several occasions.

James knew full well who I was. He showed me how to handle the shotgun but I still managed to finish the day with a huge bruise on my shoulder from the weapon's recoil. Thankfully he behaved himself and although we were both wary of each other, we parted as friends.

The royal birth got me thinking about my own family and as a hobby, in the little spare time I managed, I started to look into my family history and soon became fascinated with it. I knew all about my mother and father and my grandparents, with whom I lived in Fulham as a young girl. I also knew there were secrets in my family that have been kept hidden for many years. At one stage I commissioned a genealogist, who discovered that the lady I thought was my grandmother twice re-moved was not. My true great, great grandmother had been a theatrical actress – perhaps that's where my love of the stage originated.

The more I started digging back through my family history, the more intrigued I became. I have always known several generations back my family on my mother's side were immigrants but I never knew where we descended from. In old photos my ancestors always looked dark and my mum too was dark-skinned. Whenever we went on holiday and she sunbathed people would ask her if she was Spanish, Italian or Greek. My grandfather George was also very dark.

In the days before he died he tried to tell my sister something very important about our heritage but the details are still confused and we have never been able to discover whether or not it is true. Granddad George was on his deathbed and he was talking to my sister. He took her hand and looked at her.

'Tell your mother we are Indian,' he said.

Soon after George passed away. He was the patriarch of the family and left a huge hole. The family was in mourning and preoccupied with arrangements for the funeral and so my sister forgot about the conversation for several weeks. Then one day, about a month after George's funeral, she talked to me about it (I can't remember what it was that jogged her memory).

'Grandpa George told me something the day before he died,' she said. 'He got hold of my hand, he sat up and looked at me with his big black eyes and said, "You have to tell your mother we are from America, we are Red Indians".'

I was confused. It sounded very unlikely – we certainly didn't have Native American features. I had always believed our roots lay in the East, not the West.

'What did he actually say?' I asked.

But her memory was clouded by the events of the last weeks.

'He said Indian. He must have meant Red Indian because we can't be Asian.'

But I was sure she'd misunderstood. I believed Grandpa George had been trying to tell her a family secret on his deathbed: he was trying to tell her the truth about where we came from. I had always suspected our origins ever since I was shown a mysterious photograph when I was little.

My Great Uncle Lou lived in a place called Southfields. Today it is just another part of London but when I was a little girl it was like being in the country. He was George's brother and my mother was very close to him. She used to send me to see him. She would put me on the train from where we lived in Fulham and I'd travel a few miles down the line, where Uncle Lou would be waiting to meet me. A very tall dark man with a moustache, he looked Indian. He was married to Aunt Daisy and she never got on with his mum, my mum's grandma, because Daisy was a divorcee and my mum's gran was a devout Christian. Aunt Daisy also had had two children from her previous marriage and was a lot older than Lou. She had a face like a pug, very round with bulging eyes, but she was lovely and she treated me like a granddaughter.

When I used to visit she would often bring out the old family photograph albums. They lived in a very old, quiet house and all I could hear was the clock ticking as she leafed through the heavy pages of the bound books.

One of the photographs always caught my attention: it was a picture of two women standing in front of an aspidistra plant. The face of one of the women had been inexplicably cut out carefully but you could see her hand and she was dark-skinned.

'Why hasn't the lady got a face?' I asked.

Always I would ask why the lady didn't have a face and she would never tell me.

'Don't tell your mother we have been looking at these,' she'd say, conspiratorially.

Uncle Lou died first and Daisy and her daughter and son, who had grown up thinking they were our blood relations, kept the album. When Daisy died, it passed to her children. Mum was annoyed because she felt it belonged to her. Years later the album went missing and we never saw it again.

I'm certain the mysterious picture was of my great, great grandmother and I'm convinced she originated from the Indian subcontinent. When I try and look back with my gift and peer through the mists of time I cannot see clearly enough to know for sure. Again, my psychic ability is not meant for me. Although family have appeared to me, I cannot summon them and I can't read my past any more than I can read my future. That's why things still come as a surprise to me. And why I couldn't see the next drama in my life as it slowly began to build up without my knowledge.

In 2013 I thought my life was back on track. I was fit and healthy, I had won my court case for libel and had embarked on a sixth year of touring. Everything seemed settled. But the critics and sceptics hadn't really left me alone; they were busy in the background. Often an article or a blog or message would appear somewhere that mentioned me and called for my powers to be tested. Thankfully, since the libel case false allegations that I cheated my audiences had stopped but I was still regularly called into question. It was tiring and exasperating. I'd just been through two years of Hell, why wouldn't they leave me alone and get on with their own lives? It always appeared that I was one who was targeted. That, unfortunately, was the price of being the UK's best-known psychic, it seemed.

There was very little logic in any of the arguments being put forward. One man, a magician who had worked as a fake psychic in the past, went on TV and talked about the trickery he had used and implied that other psychics used the same techniques. It was like a dodgy roofer claiming publicly that every other roofer is dodgy just because he or she is.

For me it felt like a sustained campaign of harassment. At times I got upset but tried to brush it off as a price I needed to pay in order to help people. John got upset too. And he grew more protective – he is an old-fashioned man from an era when husbands defended their wives. He'd seen the effect the hate campaign had had on me and he'd read the threats that had been made against me. Understandably he was worried.

In 2014, people started turning up at my shows and giving out leaflets. I was first aware of it in March (John told me after a show). He had first encountered them outside a theatre in Manchester. Someone came into the foyer and told him there was a man outside, giving out leaflets. John went outside to see what was happening. There were several people with leaflets and they were trying to hand them to people going into the show. John took a copy and showed me after the show. We sent it to our lawyer, who advised us that the content repeated some of the allegations made in the libellous false story. People appeared again outside a theatre in Liverpool. This time my son-in-law Daren spoke to one of the people and asked why pick on me and my shows and not on any other psychic. The man explained that he was expressing his right to free speech. John then went out and explained to him that he'd had legal advice and that the leaflets he was giving out contained defamatory allegations.

Next a leafleter appeared outside The Shaw Theatre, which is a small theatre in London attached to a hotel. John in particular was worried – he knew how unsettling the abuse that I had received in the past had been and was worried that someone fanatical would latch onto the leaflet campaign. At the Shaw Theatre the man was leafleting the audience on the forecourt so he was asked to leave. Daren and John both went out to speak to him. John told me later that he had become involved in an argument. He didn't tell me the details, he just said he was fed up with it and that he was worried.

I didn't think about what had happened outside the theatre. According to John it was no big deal. But I did feel sorry for the audience who were being leafletted when all they were trying to do was have a nice night out. And by association I felt harassed. I wished the man would just leave me alone. It felt like I was being picked on, just as I'd been singled out and bullied at school for being different.

Chapter 25
...Into the fire

The day my life fell apart again started like any other, except I was in a hotel on the Isle of Wight. It was exactly the sort of hotel you might imagine – a bit tatty round the edges but friendly enough and half the rooms had sea views. It was grey day; it was windy. It was a Saturday in October 2014. The evening before I had performed a show and now I was looking forward to getting home. The journey back was not going to be too bad – a 30-minute ferry ride and a two-hour drive up the A3, then I'd be home. All things considered, it was an average day. I had a few calls to make, which I planned to do in the back of the car. My son-in-law Daren was with me. The day before he'd driven me over to the island, manned the merchandising stall and was, as far as I knew, in the dining room having breakfast.

A few days previously the sceptical leafleters had been at another show. They were planning a Psychic Awareness Month, during which they planned to give out yet more leaflets.

When John told me about it, I sighed.

'I wish they would just leave me alone but they are not going to give up, are they?'

It was a rhetorical question. John could see the situation was upsetting me but I had resigned myself to the fact that they would carry on regardless. I could cope – it came with the territory – but I felt bad for my fans who had used their hard-earned money to buy tickets for the shows and were having their decisions questioned. And there really wasn't anything I could do except duck in and out of theatres and hope they remained moderate and didn't encourage any people who were fanatical to follow their cause. My fans meanwhile were being stopped and questioned as they went out for a night's entertainment. It just didn't seem fair.

I didn't object to the sceptics' right to voice their opinions but through bitter experience over the years I had come to realise that some elements of the sceptic community were, ironically, extremely dogmatic and closed to discussion; they were judgemental and narrow-minded. In their opinion, if you believed in an afterlife and if you believed that some people possessed the ability to contact the afterlife, you were wrong. They were non-believers, which was their right, but they believed everyone else should be non-believers too. By the same token these people did not believe in God, Heaven or Hell. I wondered why they were not picketing churches instead but I guessed that I was an easier target.

Thankfully, there had been no sign of them on the Isle of Wight. We'd had a peaceful evening and I was relaxed and thinking absent-mindedly about the rest of the week while packing my small overnight bag when the phone rang. John's ID flashed on the screen. I answered.

'Don't panic,' he said.

As soon as anyone says that the first thing any-one does is panic – and I did.

'What's happened?' I asked quickly.

'We have a bit of a problem. It's nothing, really,' he said, flustered.

I wanted him to get to the point.

'John, just tell me what's happened,' I said.

'Someone's put a video up online.'

My immediate thought was that it was of me but I couldn't think what it could be.

'What, of me?' I asked. I was trying to work out what it could be. Even though I'd done nothing wrong, my heart was racing.

'No, it's of me,' he answered.

That really confused me. John was John; he didn't do anything controversial. Surely he hadn't been caught coming out of a hotel room with a young model?

'What is it, John? What have you done?' I asked warily.

'It's a video of the row I had with one of the leaf-leters,' he said.

Now I was confused; I'd completely forgotten about it.

'What? When?' I stuttered.

John explained that it was the row in April out-side the Shaw Theatre.

'Surely it can't be that bad,' I said to him, 'what did you do? You didn't hit him, did you? And why is it on video?'

'No, of course I didn't hit him,' replied John. 'I gave him some verbals and told him where to go. He was wearing a hidden camera. Daren is in the video too.'

'A hidden camera, why was he wearing a hidden camera?' I really couldn't understand what was going on.

'I played straight into his hands,' sighed John. 'Listen, you need to see the video. There may be some problems.'

So I arranged to meet him at the office when I got back for a crisis meeting and went down to find Daren to see if he could shed any more light on the subject. I had a deeply unsettling feeling in my stomach; I knew by the tone of John's voice that he was really worried.

When I saw Daren and he looked at me that feeling got much worse. Daren was mortified; he could barely look at me.

'What the...?' I exclaimed. 'Daren, can you tell me what's going on?'

Daren had to compose himself.

'The video's been edited. It shows John saying some nasty stuff about this bloke,' he told me.

'What kind of stuff?' I asked.

'He calls him a gay boy and a poof.'

I stopped. The words were like a slap in the face.

'You mean he's been homophobic?'

'John probably doesn't see it like that but yes, anyone who doesn't know him will look at the video and come to that conclusion. And it doesn't look good.'

But his words were not registering and what I'd been told did not have time to sink in. My phone rang: it was Hayley from the office.

'Tell me honestly, Hayley. How bad is it?' I asked.

'It's bad,' she said bluntly. 'We need to put out a statement.'

The anger started to rise in me. What had John done? As if we hadn't been through enough without him acting like an idiot.

As soon as I put the phone down, it rang again. This time it was a friend calling to offer her support.

'Oh God, what's he done?' I asked her.

'It's very unpleasant. He uses some horrible language,' she said.

On the journey back Daren hardly spoke. The ferry seemed like the longest boat ride I'd ever been on. As we crossed onto the mainland the skies got darker and more brooding and mirrored my view. The silence was only punctuated by more calls. I started to piece together the details. It was horrible; John had been vile, he'd used language that was alien to me. What he said was bigoted and threatening. Daren had been involved too. The behaviour of my husband was inexcusable. I was disgusted with him and I wanted to distance myself from him; he had let me down and he'd let his family down too.

As I learnt the full scope of the incident a hole opened inside me: it felt like grief. The John who had said those things wasn't the man I had married; I was mourning for him. Relationships are built on shared values and at that point he and I had nothing in common. If John truly believed that it was OK to use such homophobic language not only were we on different pages, we were different books.

Now I put my head in my hands and wept. I really didn't know what to do; I couldn't change what had happened but I needed to let the world know that I was no part of that vile footage.

By the time I got to the office John was there. He was sheepish and that made me dislike him even more. We both had plenty of gay friends, I wondered what they would be thinking.

The first thing I did was to draft a statement apologising for the offence caused. I made it plain that I did not condone the actions of my husband.

'Why, John,' I implored him, 'why did you do it? Why did you use that language?'

He was repentant and upset.

'I'm not homophobic, Sally, you know I'm not,' he told me.

'But, John, I would never ever use words like that, they are not even in my vocabulary. Gay people have fought against prejudice like that for hundreds of years and they still are. What were you thinking?'

John shook his head.

'I wasn't thinking, I was just trying to protect you,' he explained.

Through my website I issued a statement but I knew it was just the beginning. Already the messages of hate were starting. The power of the Internet was at work again and the story was spreading around the world. Several big news sites ran it and the comment boards began to fill up. People were rightly outraged.

The trolls had the fuel for their fire. They had a busy time that weekend. Online there were people whipping up hatred. They were extremists; they were not really sceptics, they were hate-mongers. Almost immediately the abuse and threats started up.

It was pointed out on a forum somewhere that I was playing Brighton in a few days. The seaside town is popular with the lesbian, gay, bisexual and transgender community. People started calling for a demonstration at my gig. They were also calling for John's head. And I agreed: he had never let me down so badly. I felt alone and I despised him – I didn't want to be near him, I didn't want to see his face.

When he did try and speak to me I cut him short.

'At this point, John, I really can't see a future for us.' I coughed out the words and I was serious. In my head I couldn't accept that I could ever move on.

I slept in the spare room and we didn't speak. John was worried; he skulked around the house. By the Monday I had come to a decision: in the first instance I was going to sack John and Daren.

I told Fern and she pleaded with me.

'Daren didn't do anything wrong,' she said.

But he was there and he was involved in the whole sorry affair. I felt that by having any association, I would be tainted. I wanted to make it categorically clear that John and his views had nothing to do with me and that I was as horrified by his actions as everyone else.

So I sat down and wrote a statement:

> I have come from a family background that has always been very accepting, many of my friends are gay and I have always felt happy that I am often referred to as a gay icon through my work. I am utterly ashamed and devastated at the behaviour of my husband John and son-in-law Daren and neither of them will have anything to do with my work, my business and right now, I honestly have no idea what is going to happen to my marriage.

I wrote those words with such a heavy heart. It felt like something had died inside me. John and I were a team; we'd spent our lives together and supported each other through thick and thin. We raised three beautiful children together. We were a unit, 'in sickness and in health, till death did us part'. John had been there every step of the way, from the first reading, the first bungled theatre show; the first television appearance. He'd driven me to my first appointment at Kensington Palace with the Princess of Wales; he'd warned off lunatics, he'd stood outside theatres in foyers for hours and hours. He'd faithfully followed me and helped me as I'd grown and then he'd let me down so badly I couldn't forgive him. I was sick to the stomach.

At that point, as far as I was concerned my marriage was over: I was going to divorce him. And to make matters worse he tried to defend himself. He was in as much shock as me. Over the following days there was shouting and there were rows. John slept in the other room and he stayed there for a month. I didn't have to tell him to move out of the marital bedroom, he knew just how serious things were. Our 40th wedding anniversary was fast approaching and we had arranged to renew our vows. Before it all happened we had planned a big party in the summer of 2015 to mark the occasion. The vicar from the church next to our house was going to conduct a ceremony and would bless our rings. It had always been my dream to marry John in a church but I couldn't because I was divorced. Our vicar in Surrey had been so understanding: she agreed to officiate over a proper ceremony. It was going to be like a full wedding service. But I could not imagine going through with it now.

'Are we still doing that?' John kept asking me.

'Don't even go there,' I said.

I couldn't think; I felt totally bereft because he'd said things and expressed sentiments that I just couldn't fathom.

And away from my domestic crisis things were

getting worse. Sceptics were turning up at my shows with their leaflets and fans were getting really angry with them. At one show there were six of them. Meanwhile the vile abuse and threats continued online. I became so concerned for my safety that I called in a security company. Someone online posted a threat to throw acid over me. My security advisor told me to stop doing signings and to be careful around people carrying cups and glasses. Someone even called for Jihadi John to behead me.

At the show in Brighton I had to have a bodyguard. Mercifully the planned protest did not materialise but I was advised to take precautions and go straight to my dressing room when I arrived at the venue and stay behind a locked door. There were just a few protesters. One had a placard which read, 'Ghosts demand gay rights!'.

I stepped out nervously on stage. There were a lot of gay people in the audience and I made a decision not to talk about what had happened at the beginning of the show but to mention it in the part called the wrap-up at the end, where I reviewed the evening's events.

At the end of the show I took a deep breath.

'I want to thank you all for your support. It's been a hard week and my fans have got me through...' I began.

There was a catcall from one of the boxes. I braced myself for the abuse.

A man leant over the side and shouted to me.

'Sally, listen! We've all said things we regret. Us gays can be vicious, I'm telling you it's not John's fault!'

I couldn't believe what I was hearing. With that the whole audience got up and cheered.

Choked with emotion, all I could manage was, 'Have a safe journey home. Goodnight and God bless.' I ran off stage in tears.

Over the following weeks the support from the gay community was humbling and I'll forever be thankful for the way they viewed those awful comments without the knee-jerk reaction that some did. But worse was to come.

Chapter 26
The lowest ebb

The floodgates were opened. Sacking John didn't make any difference to the trolls and whereas before all the hate had been directed at me, now it was being directed towards my family. We were all targets: John, Daren, Fern, Rebecca and me. It was awful. I felt they were paying the price for my public profile and my husband's behaviour. It was so unfair and things were about to get worse.

I could feel myself sinking back into the dark place I'd found myself in after the cheating allegations. Now I became withdrawn and depressed. And because the threats were so nasty I grew fearful too. At shows I felt totally exposed – I expected someone to jump out of the audience and attack me. Book signings were cancelled. I was advised to stay in a locked dressing room to minimise the chances of an attack. As I was ushered in and out of venues I felt like a prisoner.

One night I was at home. John was in the house too and we were barely speaking. I noticed a van drive past the front of our house very slowly. It was dark but I could see the faces of the people in the cab illuminated by the street lights. A man was driving and the female passenger was looking at our house.

I sensed something was wrong; I sensed a threat. A few minutes later the van passed again and shortly afterwards I heard footsteps on the gravel driveway. My heart was racing. The doorbell rang and John went to the door to answer.

I heard the exchange. It was a woman. She told John her car had broken down in the lane outside and did he have a spanner she could borrow? I looked out the window and recognised the woman as the passenger in the van. By the time I got to the hallway, John was already shutting the door, having realised that something was amiss.

I told him about the van.

For the rest of the night I sat listening for sounds of intruders. I left all the lights on around the house and my heartbeat quickened whenever I heard a car pass. The next day I called a security firm and got CCTV installed around the house. I felt anxious all the time and afraid in my own house; I was having a meltdown.

At the office we set up an Internet monitoring system to keep track of what was happening online. Whenever John or I were mentioned online, we would get notification. The week after the video was released, something truly disturbing happened. One of my staff noticed a Tweet that had been posted: it was a photograph of my grandsons on holiday in their swimming shorts, along with a photograph of my old house, where Fern and Daren were now living with the kids. Their cars were parked in the driveway. The

Tweet read something like 'this is where disgusting Daren lives, this is what he drives and these are his children'. The threat was implicit; it was goading people.

The office called Fern and me, and Fern called the police straight away; whoever had posted the picture had to be found and apprehended. The police were fantastic – they put Fern's house under watch and started tracing the perpetrator. I paid for a company to carry out an investigation too as it would likely be quicker than the police. My daughter had CCTV installed at her house as a matter of urgency. The boys' school was notified and told to take down any photographs of my grandsons that were on its website. Already the boys had heard comments in the playground. One boy had approached the youngest and told him: 'My dad says your dad is a racist.'

The company I employed traced the Tweet – it had been posted by a man in Canada. The authorities were notified and the company also took measures to have the Tweet removed. They also started tracing other offensive and threatening messages and alerting the people who had posted them that they were breaking the law. Slowly, the message filtered through. It cost me thousands and thousands of pounds to protect myself and my family but it was a small price to pay. I felt so guilty that my children and grandchildren had been dragged into this mess. Fern was working as a personal trainer at the time but had to stop straight away to go on tour with me as I had no one else. It affected Daren's health for months.

One night Fern confided in me. 'It messes with your head. I am suspicious of everyone, I do not want to speak to anyone. We've been under siege,' she said.

All her life she had paid the price for having a psychic mum. At school and throughout adult life whenever people realised she was my daughter they would feel it appropriate to tell her what they thought of my profession. In the end she realised it was easier not to tell them because she couldn't be bothered having to argue my case all the time. When she first met Daren she kept it quiet – she would tell him he couldn't come to the house because her mum had loads of clients. He would ask what I did and she wouldn't tell him. He must have thought I was a prostitute!

For weeks after the video she didn't go to the school because she didn't want to speak to anyone or explain it. She had already run the gauntlet after the *Daily Mail* story when she was sent vile pictures. They were disgusting, pornographic images; some crazed nut who had got hold of her email account by sending what must have been hundreds of emails to different connotations of Fern Morgan at all the main email providers.

She and Daren were terrified of revenge attacks. The week the video was leaked a strange man knocked on their door out of the blue and asked for a reading. He asked for me. Fern was on tour with me at the time. Daren said he wasn't nasty but he was worried enough to take a photo of the man.

None of us could reply to any of the online hate because as soon as we did a ripple effect would start up and more people would post messages. As soon as I put anything online, the comments would begin. I put up a photo of me holding a stocking and wishing everyone a merry Christmas.

'It's alright for you, what about people who can't afford presents?' one comment read. There was no point in replying that on the same day I took the picture I had been to the supermarket, filled a trolley up with food and given it to the church for the local food bank.

I put up a photo on my website of me with the dogs and within 15 seconds of it going live there were comments, some of them bitchy. You just couldn't win.

It affected everything. I'd had such an amazing relationship with Daren up until then but he was very upset. He felt he'd been treated unfairly. For weeks he didn't speak to me. It affected the whole family, like someone had taken a knife and stabbed us all.

John, for his part, accepted what had happened.

'You've taken early retirement,' I told him after he was sacked. So he stayed at home while I went out to work.

On one occasion he mentioned he was bored.

'Listen, mate,' I hissed, 'count yourself lucky I haven't walked out because I was going to go!'

At that time I would have gladly gone to live in a flat away from him. I had support from my friends but a lot of them didn't want to be around John. Many didn't know what to say. One person advised me to book him onto an anger management course.

'Why?' I asked. 'He's not an angry person.'

One particular fan emailed me for weeks, telling me to leave John.

'He's no good for you,' she wrote. 'I can't bear to see you with him.'

In crowds I felt exposed and I recoiled whenever people approached me; I was guarded. I saved my energy for the nights and for going on stage. On a spiritual level it didn't affect me. I felt safe and supported whenever I was communicating with spirit but I wondered if I could continue. I thought about giving it all up; I started to reconsider everything.

Psychic Awareness Month trundled on. At several shows there were people handing out leaflets. Many in the audience were annoyed. One woman took several leaflets and tore them up; others heckled and told the protesters to go away. I couldn't wait for the end of the tour and for a break at Christmas. All I wanted to do was disappear and to have some time on my own to consider the future. At home John and I were going through the motions. We'd started to talk and I hadn't moved out but I was still angry with him and I didn't know how I felt about the future.

Bad news was heaped on bad news. Before the

crisis a camera crew had come to film John and me in order to make a pilot for the proposed series. Now it was being edited and everything seemed to be progressing in the right direction. I'd been shown a teaser of the show and it looked fab. But in November 2014 I heard that plans had been shelved. It was quite obvious why: I'd been tainted by the actions of my husband and no one wanted to take the risk of putting me on television.

I didn't know how much more I could take. My stress levels were sky-high and perhaps inevitably my health started to suffer too. I wasn't eating properly; I felt weak and tired much of the time. Between shows all I did was sleep. I started to develop nagging chest pains and stomach-aches that wouldn't go away. They became progressively worse until one night on stage in Richmond I began to feel shooting pains across my chest. I struggled through to the end of the show and staggered off-stage, convinced I was having a heart attack. I had to be helped to my dressing room. The pain was so acute it felt like I was being stabbed in the chest. After a while it subsided and I went home and collapsed on the floor. The next day I went to see the doctor, who sent me for scans which confirmed that I had gallstones.

It is very common for people who have had weight-loss surgery to have gall bladder problems but I believe my condition was exacerbated by stress. When I went to see my consultant Alberic Fiennes and had further scans he confirmed my suspicions and acknowledged that the strain I'd been under would not have helped. He explained that I would need to have surgery to have my gall bladder removed and told me I needed to have this done as a matter of urgency.

I was in the last week of the tour and feeling awful. After finishing on a Friday I had a five-hour drive home. I stayed in bed for two days and was admitted to hospital on the Monday morning for surgery. But I was glad to go under to get some peace. I welcomed the warm cloak of anaesthesia as it meant I wouldn't have to think about anything for a while.

When I was released after a few days I went home and developed a dreadful cough, which turned into pneumonia. In the meantime we had cancelled the planned office Christmas party because frankly no one was in the mood to celebrate.

I was ill all over Christmas. We went to Fern's, where I had a spoonful of peas and then came home. I was so ill, I spent the rest of the day in bed. The kids tried to make it nice for me and so did John, but I was very low. As I had been working constantly since the crisis began I'd had no time to think about it all and consider the implications and in that period it all hit me. It affected everything.

I'd never felt so lost and alone and I wondered if there was a way back.

Chapter 27
Learning to love again

As the New Year approached I started to review my situation. I feared that the onslaught from the trolls and the sceptics would signal the end of my career and my calling to take my gift to the masses. I also feared that the video would mean theatres no longer wanted to book me. Thankfully those fears proved unfounded. I was given a lot of support from fans who realised although I was married to John, the sentiments he had expressed were not mine.

John also got some support. Many people who knew him realised just how out of character his outburst had been. Some of the theatre managers who had known us for years offered their support. One sent a text to John that said: 'The John in that video is certainly not the John I know, you are welcome here any time'.

A drag artist we knew posted a picture of himself and John online and wrote that John was not homophobic and that he had even spoken about going on a Gay Pride march in the past.

John and I began to talk. I realised I needed to make a decision. It was unfair to leave him hanging on, waiting to see whether or not I was going to walk out. I needed to commit to an answer. Was I going to make a go of it, or was I walking away?

I hadn't even started to figure out whether or not I could forgive him.

The epiphany came to me from spirit. It was New Year's Eve and I was asleep. A voice in a dream guided me. My grandma's words drifted through to me from somewhere at once familiar but also so far away. They led me back to life with a simple phrase. I woke at midnight with a single sentence in my head and I knew what I had to do.

Like most children, my first experience of human death was the loss of a grandparent: my grandma, Nanny Gladys. I was so young when she passed away, just four at the time, and I have no firm memories of her but I knew in the dream that it was her calling to me.

Nanny Gladys was an amazing woman who could do amazing things. It was no surprise that she had come through to me in my hour of need because Nanny Gladys had the gift too. She was a medium. She ran a newspaper stall outside Putney Bridge Underground station in south London. I never really knew her because I was so young when she died but I had snatches of memories. I remember she used to sing all the time; her voice filled the house. I remember her encouragement when I started to take my first steps and how she'd sometimes look after me in the day when Mum went to work. I had an image of her in my mind – tall and slim, hunkered down inside her padded coat, yelling the day's headlines to the commuters as they got on and off the trains.

Outgoing and sociable, she loved to pass the time of day with the people at the station, catching up on the community gossip. The world was a lot smaller then and everyone knew everyone else. Nanny Gladys was one of the linchpins of the community. If you wanted to know what Mrs Jones from the laundrette had been up to, Nanny Gladys had the gossip. If you wanted to know about the strange man who visited number 42 when the man of the house was at work, Nanny Gladys would be able to tell you. She would know things about people that she shouldn't have known. Just by brushing someone's hand when they passed her money for their evening paper she could tell deeply personal things about them. It was as if the spark of a secret had jumped from their hand to hers in that brief contact.

From what my mum told me, Nanny Gladys didn't hide the truths she knew either. If someone was up to no good she'd tell them; if they had a health problem she'd wish them well. 'Hope those piles clear up, Norma,' she'd say, and then she'd likely put a hand over her mouth in mock horror and try to hide the sparkle in her eyes. She was a mischievous one, was Gladys, and even though she upset plenty of people with her inexplicable knowledge and scared just as many as well, in our neighbourhood she was well thought of. A regular in the local pub, she would pop in every night after work for her one treat a day: a glass of Guinness. Perched on the bar stool that was always waiting for her, she'd laugh and joke with the other locals and then she would come home and make sure everyone had a hot tea.

Her funeral remains one of my earliest memories. It was the flowers that burned it into my memory: a house full of flowers, so many of them that the sweet smell was overpowering, almost intoxicating. And it was that smell that woke me from my dream as the New Year came in with her voice ringing in my ears.

'If all our faults were a pimple on our face, none of us would go out the door,' she was telling me.

It was one of her favourite phrases and I knew exactly what she was saying: she was guiding me. She was telling me that no one is perfect; that everyone deserves a second chance and John was worth fighting for. For the first time in a long while I smiled and felt the warmth of optimism glow in my chest.

'I'm going to get through this,' I thought to myself.

By that time the surgery had alleviated the pain in my chest and I had started to get my appetite back. Rested, I began to feel stronger.

The next day I mulled over Nanny Gladys's words. John wasn't perfect but neither was I. His biggest fault was that he was straight talking, often to detriment of common sense or diplomacy. He just didn't think; he didn't consider the effect of his words or his actions. I was not excusing him at all but he came from an era where political correctness did not exist, which didn't make it right but it did explain why he thought it was appropriate to use the language he had used.

I had control; it was up to me to determine the path my life was going to take. I could choose to let everything get the better of me and to walk away, or I could choose to fight. So I decided to choose the latter. I realised if I chose the former all the people who had tried to destroy me and my family over the last two years would have won. They wanted to rule my life and to tell me what I should and shouldn't be doing. And I wasn't about to let that happen. I decided to give John another chance.

Outwardly we had both changed. Our lives had changed and my appearance had changed too. Fame came at a cost, it had advantages and disadvantages, but underneath it we were still the same couple who had met at a New Year's Eve party in a grotty flat in Fulham and carved out a life together. Life changes, but on the whole people don't.

I recalled another bit of advice from a family member. My mother once told me that relationships were a balancing act and you had to balance out the good with the bad.

'If they make you more happy than sad then they are right for you,' she said.

John and I were about to celebrate our 40th wedding anniversary and in those 40 years he had made me unhappy on many occasions. I'd made him unhappy too. But on balance, we had both made each other much happier than sadder.

In January 2015 we found ourselves back in our favourite restaurant, The Dining Room in Reigate. It was owned by our friend – the celebrity chef Tony Tobin from *Ready Steady Cook*.

'What are your plans in July?' I asked John, apropos of nothing.

He shrugged.

'I was thinking of renewing our vows,' I said.

John didn't have to say anything but I could sense his relief and see the look on his face. I reached over the table and squeezed his hand.

'I don't think I forgive you yet, John. Maybe I never will. Things have changed in our relationship and we will have to adjust but we are better together than we are apart,' I told him.

It was the beginning of a new journey for both of us. But I couldn't use my gift to read our future. As I've said, I have never been able to do this so I didn't know how things were going to pan out. I didn't know if we would work things out or if it was too much of an obstacle to get over but we were on the road to recovery and it felt like the right direction to take.